Betty Ford-Smith

Pinecone Quilts

KEEPING TRADITION ALIVE
Learn to Make Your Own Heirloom

C&T PUBLISHING
Another Maker Inspired!

Text and photography copyright © 2023 by Betty Ann Ford-Smith

Photography and artwork copyright © 2023 by C&T Publishing, Inc.

Publisher: Amy Barrett-Daffin

Creative Director: Gailen Runge

Senior Editor: Roxane Cerda

Technical Editor: Debbie Rodgers

Cover/Book Designer: April Mostek

Production Coordinator: Zinnia Heinzmann

Illustrator: Linda Johnson

Map Illustrations: Emilija Mihajlov

Photography Coordinator: Lauren Herberg

Photography Assistant: Rachel Ackley

Front cover photography by Karla Respress

Quilt photography by Karla Respress unless otherwise noted

Editorial and candid photography by Betty Ford-Smith unless otherwise noted

Published by C&T Publishing, Inc., P.O. Box 1456, Lafayette, CA 94549

Library of Congress Cataloging-in-Publication Data

Names: Ford-Smith, Betty, 1951- author.

Title: Pinecone quilts : keeping tradition alive, learn to make your own heirloom / Betty Ford-Smith.

Description: Lafayette, CA : C&T Publishing, Another Maker Inspired, [2023] | Summary: "Featured inside you will find five projects to try, helpful hints to assist you along the way, and a gallery of finished quilts. This book contains the rich history of the Pinecone quilt as well as instructions on how to create your own pinecone quilt, helping to continue the tradition"-- Provided by publisher.

Identifiers: LCCN 2022061394 | ISBN 9781644032961 (trade paperback) | ISBN 9781644032978 (ebook)

Subjects: LCSH: Patchwork--Patterns. | Quilting--Patterns. | Pinecone quilts.

Classification: LCC TT835 .F6678 2023 | DDC 746.46/041--dc23/eng/20230203

LC record available at https://lccn.loc.gov/2022061394

Printed in China

10 9 8 7 6 5 4 3 2

Dedication

This book was written for Miss Sue with love and fond memories. Thank you for sharing a part of your life with me and teaching me how to make your quilt.

Acknowledgments

Thank you to my mom and dad for providing me with a wonderful life.

Thank you to Nancy Strickland Fields, Museum Director, curator, and lecturer at the Museum of the Southeast American Indian, for granting permission to use a photo of Maggie Lowrie Locklear's Pinecone Quilt and to Tyler Karpovich, Museum Specialist, for taking the photo. My appreciation to Rachael Baar, Curator of the National Quilt Museum in Paducah, Kentucky for capturing my exhibit experience on film. Thanks also go to Leslie Levy, Executive Director and Camilo Sanchez, Curator of Exhibitions for the International Quilt Museum in Lincoln, Nebraska for going above and beyond to photograph my exhibit.

Many thanks to Dr. Kristin Congdon for the constant encouragement, advice, and inspiration—you've been a very special friend for many years. I have also come to admire and appreciate all the hard work Dr. Carolyn Mazloomi has put into the world of quilting through her collection, sharing quilts with exhibits, and through more than a dozen books. Dr. Malzoomi, thank you for your encouragement to keep sewing and exhibiting my work. Thank you for sharing my work with a larger audience than I could have imagined.

Another thank you goes to all my friends who I've shared pictures and stories with over the years—thank you for enduring my constant photo journals and continuing to say, "You should write a book." Huge appreciation and gratitude to Katell Renon for sharing my work on your blog and keeping my story alive in France and across the world. Racheldaisy, you lifted my spirits in the middle of the night when I was feeling down and overwhelmed while completing this book, and you continue to inspire me with your bright colors, cheerfulness, suggestions, and gifts. Kathy Wallace, many thanks for suggesting that I needed a website and for putting it together so people could find me.

Thank you to Karla Respress for taking such fabulous pictures at all hours of the day and for squeezing me into your very busy schedule for almost a year and also to Kenny Meza Photography for your skilled drone work and for patiently waiting for the wind to die down.

Thank you to my husband, Butler H. Smith Jr., for his patience, understanding, and encouragement.

Finally, my tremendous respect and appreciation go to Roxane Cerda, who kept me on her watch list for eight years. She convinced me that my book would be something people would want to read and encouraged me to keep working on it.

Contents

Foreword   6

Introduction   8

Miss Sue: A Master Craftswoman   10

Meeting Miss Sue   11

Her Early Years   16

Quilting with Miss Sue   17

The Gee's Bend Experience   21

The Research Experience   26

A Brief History and Cultural Origins   32

Connections Across the South   34

   The Pinecone in Gee's Bend   34

   The Larger Southern Area   36

Other Artistic Expressions   38

North Carolina Lumbee River Area   38

African Connections   40

Sharing the Tradition   44

Gallery of Vintage and Contemporary Pinecone Quilts   51

Vintage Quilts   52

Contemporary Quilts   60

Make Your Own Pinecone Quilt   78

Tools   79

Fabrics   80

Basic Technique   81

Binding   84

Pinecone Projects to Get You Started   86

Puffy Pinecone Pillow   87

Pinecone Baby Quilt   90

Pretty Pinecone Corsage   93

Striking Pinecone Hoop Wall Art   95

Gee's Bend-Inspired Patchwork Pine Burr
Quilt   98

Further Reading   102

Books   102

Other Resources   102

About the Author   103

Foreword

After meeting an active and elderly quilter in 2004, Betty Ford-Smith became fascinated with the Pinecone quilt. In this book, she introduces the reader to her journey with a then-little-known quilting practice, a folded, circular, and layered quilt, rooted in various traditional cultures. Known by several names, today, this quilting technique is becoming more visible, thanks to Betty's diligent work in keeping the tradition alive.

Betty's mentor was a 92-year-old woman everyone called Miss Sue. A mother of twelve children, she lived not far from Betty's home in Sebring, Florida. Long interested in traditional African American art, Betty embraced Miss Sue's teachings which she is now passing on to other quilters. Readers of this book will learn about her friendship with Miss Sue, the cultural roots of the pinecone quilt, and possible connections to the colorful paintings of the artist Alma Thomas. Betty also identifies a region in Alabama, close to the borders of Georgia and Florida, that may have been a center for the pinecone quilt and an inspiration for Thomas' paintings.

Additionally, readers will be introduced to several quilters, including Bettie B. Selter and China Grove Myles (African American quilters from Gee's Bend, Alabama), Maggie Lowrie Locklear (a Lumbee quilter from North Carolina), and Addie Bullock (an African American quilter from Marianna, Florida).

Betty then takes the reader through a detailed process of making a quilt and smaller, less demanding projects using the pinecone technique. Her instructions are encouraging, with helpful hints noted throughout the step-by-step process. If the needle doesn't easily go through the layered fabric, she suggests a solution. If a tuck is difficult to understand, she provides a second way to grasp the technique. And if the process seems too challenging at times, she provides encouragement. In every section, Betty's love for the quilting process and teaching comes through.

Pinecone quilts, which are thick and heavy, are more difficult to make than most other quilt forms. Yet, under the adventuresome eyes of Miss Sue and Betty, they are mesmerizingly beautiful.

After learning to make Miss Sue's way of creating a Pinecone quilt, Betty became unstoppable. She began teaching the process in workshops all over the country and in France. She started receiving commissions and invitations to exhibit her work. Tirelessly, she kept at it, teaching hundreds of other quilters with inspiration and patience.

Betty is not only a quilter and a teacher, she is also a collector. When I first visited her in her home over fifteen years ago, I was stunned by the quality and quantity of her art collection. Works from Africa, Haiti, and the African American South were displayed everywhere on walls, steps, tables, chairs, and beds. The tour was breath-taking. But when I got to the garage and experienced Miss Sue's quilts and dresses, I was stopped in my tracks. Here was color and movement unlike anything I had seen before in a quilt, and her dresses, re-constructed from flea market purchases, took risks in patterning that I found surprisingly fresh.

For at least a decade now, Betty has regularly been sending me emails with multiple photos of quilts, exhibitions, and workshops. She's always involved in passing on the tradition, one way or another.

Beautifully illustrated, *Pinecone Quilts: Keeping Tradition Alive, Learn to Make Your Own Heirloom* is just what it says it is, a history and how-to book. But more than that, it's about making connections, to fabric, history, and the quiet delight of piecing together colors and patterns. This is a book that takes you on Betty's journey and begins one of your own.

Kristin Congdon
Professor Emerita, Philosophy and Humanities
University of Central Florida

Introduction

The quilts I make are most commonly called Pinecone, Pine Burr, or Cuckleburr quilts, but I've also seen them called Pineapple, Prairie Point, Bull's Eye, and Target quilts. Years ago, before I knew what Pinecone quilts were, I'd seen an amazing historic quilt by Maggie Lowrie Locklear of the Native American Lumbee Tribe of North Carolina. Her *Pinecone Patchwork Quilt* was, and still is, on exhibit at the Museum of the Southeast American Indian. Though the exhibit included pinecone imagery that was used on clothing and jewelry for many Lumbee celebrations, I was particularly amazed by her quilt and immediately wanted to learn how to make one.

Finding out where something originated can be very challenging, but I was determined. Was it one of a kind? Or, if there were many more quilts of this pattern out there, who was making them and what were they called? I lucked out, and the first person to show me a contemporary Pinecone quilt also introduced me to Miss Sue, the woman who would eventually show me how to make these quilts.

Arlene Dennis, a colorful, creative, perky African American woman known as Miss Sue, taught me how to design and construct this type of quilt when she was 92 years old. When she died at 98, Miss Sue was still making Cuckleburr quilts, as she called them. When she was young, her family moved to Bainbridge, Georgia, where she had and raised her twelve children. Later, she moved to Florida—first to Tallahassee, then Quincy, and eventually to Sebring, where we met. While living in Quincy, Florida, and Bainbridge, Georgia, she made many Cuckleburr quilts to help keep her family warm. Although her grandmother had passed the craft down to her, Miss Sue did not pass it on to her own children. I was honored that she taught me to make these beautiful quilts.

I feel privileged that Miss Sue passed this quilting tradition on to me and I feel that it is important that it not be lost. My effort to share this traditional art form with a new generation has led me to travel the world. I've journeyed internationally to conduct workshops to teach all who have been willing to listen and learn. Both learning and teaching the skills to make these Pinecone quilts has shown me that it does not matter where you come from, your economic position in life or religious beliefs, the cultural or ethnic identity you have, or what language you speak. Quilters share a collective language—a patchwork of love, acceptance, and sharing. Through this book, I hope to share this tradition and its origins with you.

The very first Pinecone
quilt I completed under
Miss Sue's mentorship

Miss Sue: A Master Craftswoman

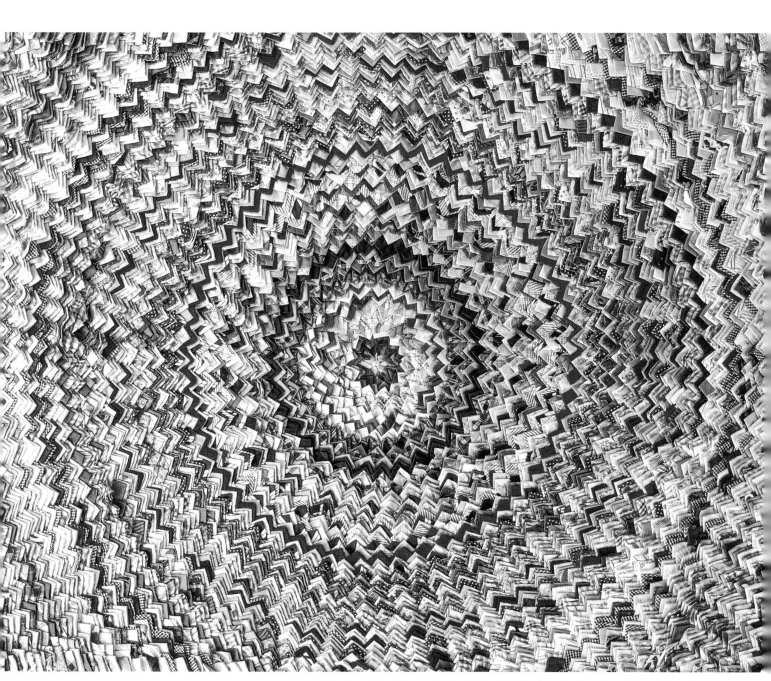

The Long Way Home, 90″ × 65″, c. 1990s, hand pieced by Arlene Dennis
Photo by Kenny Meza

I snapped a picture of the first contemporary Pinecone quilt I ever saw in person so I could try to learn more.

Meeting Miss Sue

In 2004, while I was vending at a cultural street festival, a recent acquaintance, Linda, stopped by and said she had something in the trunk of her car to show me. She opened the trunk and inside were two of the most unusual quilts I had ever seen. I immediately wanted to know what they were called, where she got them, how much they cost, and if there were more. I became even more curious when she seemed reluctant to tell me exactly where she got them. She did share that the 92-year-old quilter who made them called them Cuckleburr quilts.

I was instantly taken by the handwork, the hundreds of little pieces of fabric, and the patience and time a project like this must have taken. The fact that a 92-year-old woman was still hand-sewing quilts was amazing to me and I just had to meet her. All of the people over 90 that I'd ever met could tell some interesting stories about years past, but they were neither living independently nor still involved in making their craft. I was so hopeful for the possibility of being introduced to this unbelievable woman.

Intrigued, I started researching right away. Two days later, as luck would have it, I discovered a picture online that looked a lot like the Cuckleburr quilt, but it was called a Pinecone quilt. I'd only seen quilts like this in person once so I was not sure I was looking at the right design. I searched for hours with no luck. It wasn't until I decided to specifically type in "African American quilts" that I found a quilt for sale that was similar to the ones in Linda's trunk. The seller indicated that it was at least 100 years old and had been made by a 90-year-old blind woman. Of course, the seller was asking a great deal of money for this quilt, which was not in my budget. I was hitting dead ends and called Linda to ask for another look at her quilts.

It was December of 2004 and I was trying to stay busy so Christmas wouldn't be so depressing. I'd lost my mother a year and a half before, and I was missing her terribly. I had some new friends and needed a new direction in life. I was working as an educator, and when Christmas vacation started, I finally got my wish to meet Miss Sue, the little 92-year-old woman who was still sewing every day.

Detail of *Antique Pine Burr Quilt with Blue Sashing*, 82″ × 65″, c. 1950–1960
Photo by Kenny Meza

When I arrived at Miss Sue's house, I saw the sign that had prompted Linda to stop in the first place. I'd been passing that house with its colorful, junk-filled yard every day for two years, but I had never noticed the sign until now. I got out of the car and went in for my first meeting with Arlene Dennis, affectionately known as Miss Sue. I'd later understand what a compliment it was that I was invited in right away. The house was dimly lit and filled with knickknacks that had been neatly and purposefully placed on every wall, shelf, and table. The fireplace had quilt-patterned contact paper pasted all over the bricks, which made the hearth very cozy-

looking, and it seemed like a special sign of her craft. I had so many questions that I did not know where to begin, but I was very sure I wanted Miss Sue to teach me how to make her Cuckleburr quilts.

Miss Sue agreed to teach me, and we started the very next day. Luckily, it was still Christmas break, so I had time off. I went to her house every day for two to three hours and sat in front of the fireplace with her, sewing and talking. Miss Sue told me it would take some time for me to finish a king-size quilt, but I was determined to do so in two months. We started our quilts at the same time so I could watch her, learn, and try to keep up. My fingers would get sore and my eyes tired in her dimly lit house, but it was fun sitting in front of that contact paper–faced fireplace. Every day, she dipped snuff and told me stories about her life. I was soaking up this special adventure while working hard to complete my quilt. It was often very hot in the house, but I managed to keep going every day and I completed my quilt at the same time that Miss Sue finished hers.

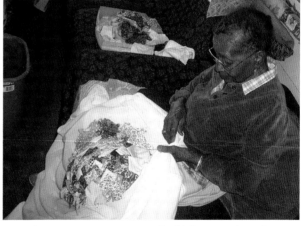

Miss Sue just starting a new Cuckleburr quilt on her front porch

During this time, the local newspaper learned about Miss Sue. I was concerned that all the attention might tire her out, but she loved every moment of it. She liked it so much that I decided to take her to the school where I worked so the students could meet a local quilter.

On a warm afternoon in February 2005, I picked up Miss Sue and took her to the local high school for Black History Month. We brought a few quilts to share, including the one I'd just finished. It had taken me three months to complete and I couldn't wait to show off both the quilt and my quilting teacher, who stood next to me.

The students were amazed by what she shared. Miss Sue told the students that she was born in Quincy, Florida, in 1912, the only girl of ten children. Her parents lived on a farm, but her mother did not want her growing up to work in the fields, so she helped around the house and learned to sew sitting by her grandmother's side. She told them about how she and her grandmother made Cuckleburr quilts with scraps of fabric from old clothes that could no longer be worn, old sheets, tablecloths, leftover scraps from new clothes that were being made, curtains, or fabric that was given to them.

As she grew up, Miss Sue made all her own clothes and helped to make clothes for the family. When a student asked if she ever used a sewing machine, she said that she knew how but preferred to sew by hand. She told the students about the old quilting frame that had hung from the ceiling of a room and how she and her grandmother would lower it to make patchwork quilts by hand.

Miss Sue made more than just Cuckleburr quilts. Here, she was working on her take on a nine-patch quilt.

She explained that the process of making a Cuckleburr quilt requires hours of ripping or cutting fabric into little squares, which are then folded and hand-sewn onto a sheet one piece at a time. Not all of the fabric was gathered at the beginning. Sometimes she waited for weeks before she could continue sewing because there were no more useful scraps in the house. She did not plan the colors but carefully selected each piece and somehow would get the colors to blend and match. Each quilt was truly unique. She'd also stop for days at a time to sew something easier because her fingers would get sore and cut from pushing the needle through so many layers of cloth. Miss Sue called Cuckleburr quilts "lap quilts" (by which she meant a quilt made while holding them on your lap), which get very heavy as they near completion. Her shoulders would get sore from turning a quilt in her lap as it got heavier and heavier. A finished quilt can weigh anywhere from 18 to 28 pounds, depending on the size and the fabrics used! I was astounded that a little 5-foot-tall, 92-year-old woman could still make such heavy quilts!

The students were impressed by the colors, the weight, the fine pattern of hand-sewn stitches that can be seen on the back, and all the tiny little triangles that create the quilt's circular pattern. Likewise, these quilts never cease to amaze me. It takes a great deal of patience and three to five months of working nearly every day to finish a single quilt.

I went over to visit with Miss Sue almost every day, and every day she was sewing something. She made dresses, slips, nightgowns, tablecloths, placemats, patchwork bedspreads, curtains, dresses for little girls, baby quilts, and patchwork quilts in addition, of course, to Cuckleburr quilts. On Sundays, Miss Sue read the Bible, listened to gospel music on her radio, and did crossword puzzles while sitting on her porch. Many days, we sat and talked about her early life in Georgia, which was eventful and fascinating to hear about.

Judging from some of her stories, Miss Sue had a hard life.

Miss Sue didn't limit her craft or her use of the pinecone motif to just quilts.
Alongside quilts and clothing, Miss Sue also made hand-tufted rugs.

Her Early Years

Miss Sue was only five when her daddy taught her how to make moonshine in the fireplace. He'd lift her onto a box and let her pour and mix the ingredients in a big pot and stir until it was ready. Miss Sue said she did well in school and in the third grade was asked to teach some of the younger children. She attended school through middle school when she dropped out due to pregnancy.

She told me that all of her children were born in Bainbridge, Georgia, the first when she was just thirteen years old. Her mother was worried that she was too young to have a baby. She had the baby anyway, but her grandma took the baby and Miss Sue was only allowed to nurse and clean her; no other contact was allowed. At fifteen she became pregnant again. Miss Sue's mother had remarried and also became pregnant and Miss Sue nursed both babies—hers and her mother's.

At the age of seventeen, she married Henry Stackhouse, the son of a preacher whom she'd met at church, and they had two children together. Henry moved them onto a farm where he taught her how to raise chickens and hogs, how to build things, how to keep a garden, and how to plow with a mule. Miss Sue went on to have two miscarriages and several more children; all the while, her grandma would walk a mile and a half through the woods to bring the kids she had been raising to see Miss Sue, their mother. I listened to many stories about her life, about the twelve children she had, and how she had outlived all but one of them.

Over the course of her life, she also had a variety of occupations, from being a housewife and church secretary to doing domestic work on a farm in Tallahassee, Florida. Miss Sue also worked in a pecan factory, a tobacco plant, and a crate factory.

Miss Sue's life was marked by drama, violence, and tragedy.

Henry's sister, Beauty, brought Miss Sue's six-year-old daughter, Arnell, to visit. Arnell was sitting on the porch with Miss Sue when she was suddenly struck by lightning. Arnell died instantly. The lightning hit the house so hard that it also knocked the quilting frame off the ceiling. Maggie Pearl Williams, Miss Sue's oldest daughter, was shot by a man in St. Petersburg, Florida, who was then sentenced and sent to prison. This same man had previously murdered his own mother with a pair of scissors and spent time behind bars. Miss Sue's son Luther tragically died in a car accident while coming to visit her when he was only twenty years old.

Miss Sue often talked about the loss of a friend who died in a car accident in New York while she, herself, was driving. Miss Sue had been drinking and after that, she never drank again. She also told me about the time a man in Florida stabbed her in the head with a knife and how she shot him to protect herself. He died in her yard. This event was so unforgettable that many adults who had been kids in the neighborhood still remember that day. I recall some of them telling me they remember seeing the man hanging over the fence and Miss Sue walking down the street covered with blood, a knife sticking out of her head. The neighborhood kids remained afraid of her and never wanted to pass by her house again. She told me she did not spend any time in jail because she'd acted in self-defense. She even showed me the scar on her scalp. Miss Sue told me she could protect herself and, in fact,

shared that even in her 90s, she slept with a pistol and a set of brass knuckles in her bed.

Miss Sue seemed destined for a very long life. Her mother, Viney Jackson Butler, died at 105 or 106 years old, and her grandmother, Ammie Smart, at 102. Miss Sue survived a tough life and became a wise and independent elderly lady.

Quilting with Miss Sue

Miss Sue maintained a good, running, registered car, but she would have someone else drive her everywhere she wanted to go. She also had a motorized chair she used to get to the local flea market or the nearby dollar store on her own. One day, it got stuck on the railroad tracks and she had to be saved by a stranger from an oncoming train. I sometimes took Miss Sue shopping for groceries or to the thrift stores to hunt for good bargains on fabric. She really took her time when she got out shopping or did other errands. Each sheet she selected as a base for a Cuckleburr quilt was given the once over for thickness and wear because if the sheet was too thick, the needle couldn't pass through the layers.

The fabric also had to pass her softness test. Miss Sue would feel each piece until she believed she had just the right piece of fabric. Sometimes, I would get a little tired of this ritual, but it too was a learning experience. Now I find myself doing the same thing!

My very first lesson with Miss Sue. She started me out on a king-size sheet!

Like most of us, Miss Sue loved a good bargain, and free fabric is the best bargain of all. Sometimes the wives of local shopkeepers who were fond of and respected Miss Sue would drop off boxes of fabric. When they could not get there themselves, they would send their husbands with large barrels of trim and scrap fabrics. Sometimes it would take Miss Sue a month to go through all these scraps. Her eyes would twinkle and she would smile so big that her gold teeth would sparkle. She loved it.

It was then I realized what a compliment it was that I was invited inside on my first visit. The same men and women who brought her fabric scraps would bring her food from time to time, especially the hunters. I remember being there when people came to the house with turtle, rabbit, cow's head, fish, fruit, and pies. They would always stop at the gate and holler from the car, "Hey Miss Sue, you in there?" They knew she was either on the porch or, if the door was open, inside sewing and watching TV. They wouldn't get out of the car unless she answered, and then they would ask permission to enter her yard. They rarely came inside the house unless the gift was too heavy for Miss Sue to carry. They would take it as far as the porch and visit in the yard with her for about 15 minutes, never sitting down, and then leave.

Everyone in the neighborhood knew Miss Sue and her yellow house on the corner. Her yard was filled with artificial flowers, all neatly arranged and some featuring glued-down toy figurines as added decoration. There were several disheveled woodpiles, a few sheds where she stored her quilts, and an area with a barbed-wire fence around a dog house. At one point, code enforcement threatened to fine Miss Sue for having too much wood and other junk in her yard. Though I was very willing to help out, it was clear to me that she and I could not do the clean-up by ourselves. I was familiar with the community service work done by the local Reserve Officers' Training Corps (ROTC) battalion and thought this might be a perfect project for them. They came out and did a fantastic job! The local newspaper printed a great story about the ROTC and Miss Sue. It also resulted in the battalion informally adopting Miss Sue by checking on her and getting her firewood from time to time. Even though this was central Florida, Miss Sue burned wood in her fireplace almost every morning and, often, throughout the whole day during cooler months.

Miss Sue's yellow house on the corner. She surrounded herself with color.

During the six years we had together, Miss Sue and I mostly sat in her small, crowded, often overheated but still comfy living room. Miss Sue did her sewing from her special plastic rocking lawn chair, the kind with the plastic woven seat and back. That was the only seat she would sit in, and no one else ever sat there. She kept a big pot next to her feet to spit her snuff in and on the side, gin boxes to hold her fabric squares. Miss Sue did everything in that chair, including watching

TV, cutting vegetables to cook for dinner, and doing crossword puzzles. Sometimes she sat on her front porch to sew and occasionally she sat lower down in the yard at street level. She did not allow many people to visit on the covered porch, but from time to time she did allow people to sit outside on her lawn with her. She often stood at the fence talking to folks or would speak to them from the screened porch while they stood at the fence. I loved the times we'd sit outside to sew and talk about the good old days.

Sitting in this chair, Miss Sue would do everything from preparing meals to working on her latest quilt.

Miss Sue was a bit of a character. The screen of her porch was black, so she could see folks but they could not see her. She got a big kick out of watching people pass by and overhearing their conversations. At one point, she was making a beautiful Cuckleburr quilt for me. We'd worked out a fair deal on how much I was to pay and I checked on the progress often with the gleeful anticipation of having my very own Miss Sue quilt. One day, I didn't see it anymore. Knowing that she only worked on one quilt at a time, I asked Miss Sue about mine and she sheepishly smiled. She had sold it to someone else who offered her more money. While I was very disappointed, I knew that Miss Sue could be a bit devious at times, so I put it behind us and continued to enjoy the good things about her. I did eventually get several quilts made by Miss Sue.

I'd been learning how to make Cuckleburr quilts with Miss Sue for six years and could see she was slowing down a little with her quilt production. But at age 98, she still cooked for herself, planted her own vegetable garden, made her bed every day, and cleaned the house. Miss Sue even made her own dresses. She washed clothes in a washing machine and used the dryer or hung them on the line to dry, including her sneakers. I never saw dishes in her sink. She was still doing more at 98 than many of us do at a much younger age.

Miss Sue in her garden, doing more for herself at nearly 100 than many people do at any age.

Miss Sue taught and nurtured my Pinecone quilting development in many ways. During our time together, I made two large Pinecone quilts, compared with her four. Some of the knowledge she passed down to me was technical—components like selecting a large sheet, folding a square of fabric twice to make a triangle, using a basting stitch, and many more. I also learned a lot by just watching and observing—things like how she used her love for color and design in her environment, in her craft work, and even in what she wore. The dresses Miss Sue made and wore had mixed and matched patterns. Somehow, though, the bright colors and different prints complemented each other. There was a rhythm and a balance that was not accidental. Even the way she arranged dresses on the clothesline to dry showed her talent for creative order. She had a keen eye for delightfully artistic things.

In addition to Pinecone quilts, Miss Sue made all of her own dresses—and undergarments!

Miss Sue was abundantly creative, even though she did not have an abundance of money or social status.

When Miss Sue died in 2010 at 98 years old, she was still making these quilts entirely by hand. I later found the last quilt she made in the street on a rain-soaked pile next to her house. That encouraged me even more to do as much as I could to spread her knowledge and keep the tradition alive.

Miss Sue all dressed up, ready to go out to dinner for her birthday. This was the last restaurant meal we had together.

The Gee's Bend Experience

Rail Fence, 84″ × 87″, 2008, hand pieced and quilted by Bettie B. Seltzer

At the time I learned about the Gee's Bend quilters of Alabama, they had been getting a great deal of attention for some time. Beginning in the mid-1960s, the works of Gee's Bend quilters were being displayed and sold up north in New York. They appealed to important mainstream museums, famous collectors, and even fancy department stores because they were seen as exotic, African American folk art. The popularity of Gee's Bend quilts fluctuated, and they did not always maintain the same level of notoriety in high art circles. But, after 40 years, Gee's Bend—and the quilts, the women, their work, and the cooperative—returned to being celebrated. They were studied, exhibited, and written about in very formal and scholarly ways. Instead of being considered quaint, Black, folk art creations from rural Alabama, Gee's Bend quilts are now officially considered a part of the major American modern art movement. The U.S. Postal Service even created a custom stamp collection that celebrated Gee's Bend quilts. My husband, who was working at the post office at the time, showed me the colorful stamp books with images of quilt designs.

I told my husband we needed to go to Alabama to meet some of the women and see these quilts. A friend in Alabama invited us to stay at her house for a week and she took us on a day trip to Gee's Bend. It was March 2008, and we had an unforgettable experience. We went to the co-op building that had been built for the new Gee's Bend Quilting Collective, an organization that was established in 2003 to help women market their quilts. I'd become familiar with how these quilts looked hanging in museums, but this was very different. When we walked into the co-op, quilts were stacked along three walls from floor to ceiling and folded on metal shelves set up throughout the room. The colors were so overwhelming that it was difficult to decide which quilt was my favorite. It was also hard to see the pattern of each unless you unfolded every quilt you might have had an interest in—and that would have taken hours just to choose one. I was hoping to find some Pinecone quilts, but I did not see any. We were overwhelmed by the unbelievable number of stacked quilts. After looking at so many, we fell in love with all of the colorful quilts. Picking one seemed impossible.

With so many quilts to choose from, making a decision was tough.

Bettie B. Seltzer, one of the Gee's Bend quilters, invited us to her home to show us some of her vibrant quilts. When we walked through her house, we were surprised to see that her quilting frame was two sawhorses and that she sat in a plastic lawn chair while quilting, which reminded me of Miss Sue sitting in her lawn chair every day to quilt in front of the fireplace. Bettie had a lot of beautiful chickens in the yard and during the day, when she was not working, she loved to sit on her front porch watching the chickens, her grandchildren playing, and the neighbors coming and going. There was a good bit of activity in and around Bettie's home. Some of the interior walls of her house displayed quilts that were perhaps for sale.

Miss Sue kept all of the quilts she made outside in three metal sheds, wrapped in large black plastic bags, and she took them out one at a time when she needed to show or sell them.

The only quilt that stayed in Miss Sue's house was the one she was currently working on.

Rail Fence, 84″ × 87″, 2008, by Bettie B. Seltzer

Detail of *Rail Fence*

Made By Bettie B. Seltzer March 18-2008

Bettie stored the majority of her quilts in a cedar-lined room. As soon as I entered it, the smell reminded me of a cedar-lined hope chest. The quilts were folded neatly in two or three stacks. There was no shelving; instead, one quilt rested on top of another and the stack reached from the floor to the ceiling with just a few quilts on the bed. Like Miss Sue, Bettie sold her quilts from her home, but unlike Miss Sue, Bettie's work was supported by a national, well-regarded cooperative of women who knew each other.

There were so many quilts to choose from, we were like kids in a candy store who knew they couldn't buy all the candy. Bettie and my husband had a lot in common. She worked as the postmaster in the little post office in the town of Boykin, Alabama. They spoke at length about their jobs and hard work at the post office for some time before we finally decided on which quilts to purchase. Making

our minds up was difficult, but we finally decided on two: a red and white quilt and a multicolored quilt. The red and white quilt first caught my eye because I had recently read about the history of red and white quilts and the importance of having one in your collection. My husband loved it too because it had a touch of blue and was very patriotic. It reminded him of the military and seeing the boats on the water from the beach in Massachusetts. The second quilt I selected had a great deal of color and although it looked a little traditional, I liked that the rail fence block pattern could be clearly interpreted. It has colorful, wide sets of four strips alternating directions on each block. We didn't have enough money to buy two quilts at one time, but Bettie insisted that we pay for one but take them both and then send a money order to her when we returned home to Florida. She signed and dated each quilt.

Detail of *Red and White Ships* (see full quilt image on next page)
Notice that one of the ship's sails is facing the wrong way? Some superstitious quilters
will add a deliberate mistake to keep the devil away.

Red and White Ships, 111″ × 96″, 2008, by Bettie B. Seltzer

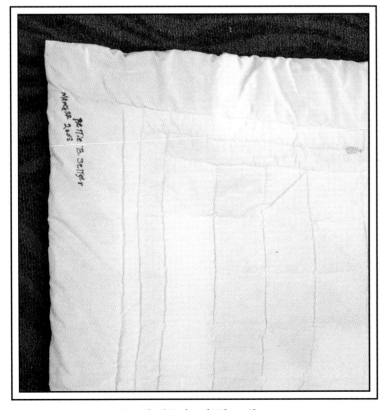

Detail of *Red and White Ships*

Bettie Seltzer was a very generous, kind, and talented quilter. I sent her copies of the pictures we took of her and her grandchildren, the chickens, and some photographs of my own quilts. We kept in touch and though Bettie became ill and weak, we were still able to talk on the phone with her children who were assisting her. In our last conversation, she told me that her cousin, Lucy Mingo, born in 1931, was the one woman in Gee's Bend that made Pinecone quilts, which Lucy called Pine Burr quilts. Lucy made small pinecone blocks and then pieced them all together. A quilt constructed like that can take two and a half years to complete. Bettie passed away in 2017.

I told Miss Sue all about my visit to Gee's Bend and about how Lucy Mingo made her quilts in little blocks first and then sewed them together. Miss Sue laughed and said that was too much work, starting over and over again when you could make one large circle. So, I continued to make the large circles the way she taught me. I eventually decided to give it a try and made one Pine Burr quilt using twelve blocks composed of smaller pieces with sashing between the blocks. You can find a variation of this quilt, the Gee's Bend–Inspired Patchwork Pine Burr Quilt, in the projects chapter of this book (page 98).

The Research Experience

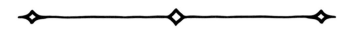

Photo by Akerri / Shutterstock.com

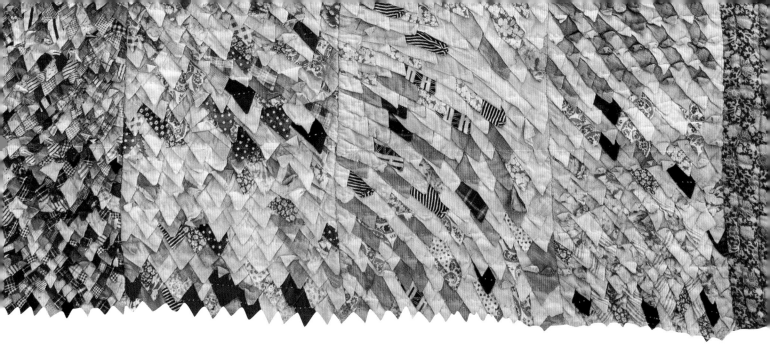

Intrigued by Maggie Lowrie Locklear's quilt at the Museum of the Southeast American Indian at the University of North Carolina at Pembroke (page 39), I began searching for origins and influences. Initially, I started looking through all the quilt books and quilt magazines in my house, but there was nothing that looked quite right. I turned to the internet, but I did not really know what I was looking for because the type of quilt I wanted to find was not easy to describe.

In 2004 I began to search for books containing actual pictures of the Pinecone quilt and eventually spent eighteen years trying to piece together its origins. At the beginning of my research, while I did find photos of what I knew to be Pinecone quilts, I could not find the name Cuckleburr or Pinecone that referred to a quilt design with concentric circles made of folded fabric triangles, then filled in to make four corners for a square or rectangular finish. The Pinecone quilt is still unknown to most people. I have extensive experience showing my work in gallery exhibits and at cultural art festivals and, still, many people have never seen a Pinecone quilt.

My more formal research journey began when I finally came across actual images of Pinecone quilts in several books. Up to that point, my searches hadn't even resulted in finding the name Pinecone quilt, or even Cuckleburr or Pine Burr. I had not yet found an example that matched the quilts I'd seen. I eventually found three books that served me well on my search for more knowledge.

Florida Quilts encouraged me to look for further examples of Pinecone quilts and *The Freedom Quilting Bee: Folk Art and the Civil Rights Movement in Alabama* sent me to Gee's Bend and expanded my understanding of Pinecone quilts and the history of Southern African American quiltmakers. The third book, *Southern Quilts: Celebrating Traditions, History, and Designs* was quite informative too, but my reaction to reading it is what began my journey of handing down this technique to anyone willing to learn.

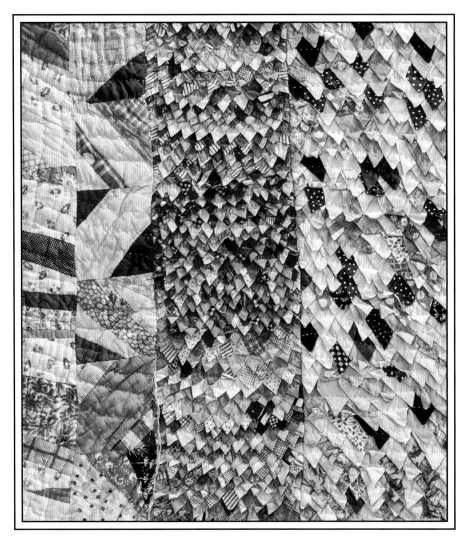

Detail of *Antique Prairie Point Quilt*, 68″ × 75″, c. 1940s, quilter unknown
Similar to some of Addie Bullock's quilts, this antique quilt features rows of
pinecone triangles facing down toward the bottom of the quilt.
Photo by Kenny Meza

I finally spotted that first picture of a Pinecone quilt in *Florida Quilts* by Charlotte Allen Williams. The picture shows a quilt made in 1966 by Addie Bullock, an African American woman living in Marianna, Florida. The book didn't give a lot of information—it had just the photo and two short paragraphs. However, the author did mention that this quilt was called a Pinecone quilt and was uncommon. The author explained that the pinecone-like pattern was typically formed from square fabric pieces folded into triangles, with each triangle stitched down to eventually result in a series of concentric circles. Addie's quilt itself was a bit of a different Pinecone quilt: Her design method included two additional vertical rows of prairie points going up and down two sides of the quilt.

Florida Quilts also mentioned the heavy weight of Pinecone quilts as the result of the ten or more thicknesses of fabrics stitched through to achieve the pattern. That was something I certainly knew about from my own experience in making those first two quilts with Miss Sue. Although there was just one Pinecone quilt in *Florida Quilts*, this find was key to my research goals. I'd finally seen one in a book and with just enough of a description to confirm, "Yes, this is what I've been looking for!"

Reading Nancy Callahan's *The Freedom Quilting Bee* prompted me to really think about how history and race were connected to the quilting craft and vice versa. I saw how quilts can be records of connections between history and racial matters, but also how quilts are artifacts that can connect people to each other. By that, I mean they can connect more than just family members to each other.

Quilts can connect people within communities and across districts, states, regions of the country, and even beyond.

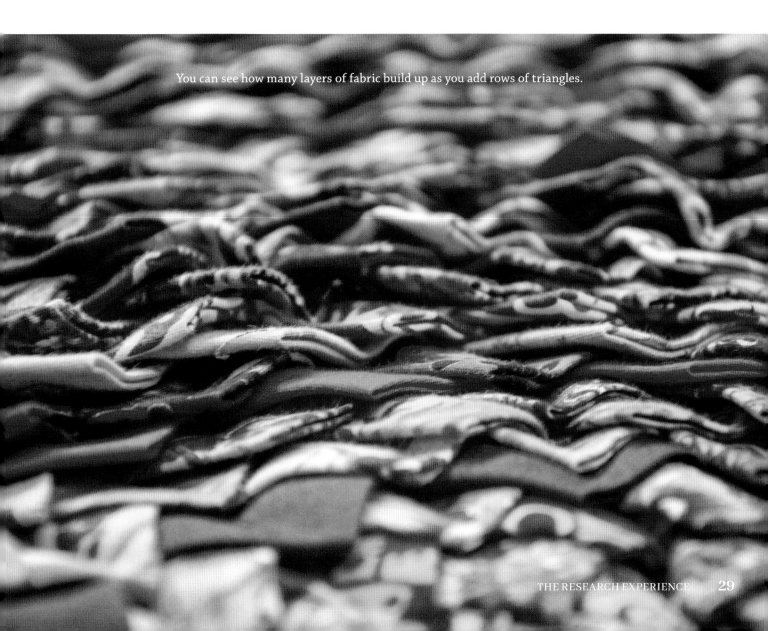

You can see how many layers of fabric build up as you add rows of triangles.

Gee's Bend is near Selma, Alabama, and is part of the Black Belt region, a term that originally referred to the richness of the soil, though as a result of the aftermath of the plantation system is now a more generalized term for a region with a majority Black population. When quilters in Wilcox County, which includes Gee's Bend, organized into the remarkable Freedom Quilting Bee, it was the mid-1960s and the height of the Civil Rights Movement. The Freedom Quilting Bee helped Black women quilters to market their work, but the idea for the cooperative was introduced by and organized along with, white outsider advocates whose original mission was to uphold voting rights. That original political purpose resulted in some social and economic benefits beyond just those for the quiltmakers and their craft. One example is the Freedom Quilting Bee's purchase of 23 acres of land, which made it possible for eight families that had previously been evicted to then buy some of the land and become independent landowners.

As a result of this exchange between Alabama communities and outside influencers, the quilts were taken to the large southern cities of Atlanta and Houston, then found their way north to New York City. Colorful, strikingly patterned quilts made in Gee's Bend and the surrounding area were being sold in northern high-end stores and at auctions and displayed and sold at museums. Gee's Bend quilts came from generations of African American women passing down their skills, and now the quilts and the stories of these women were being shared with a wider audience.

Although, as a collector, I already knew it, Callahan's book did remind me of how quilts are also like pages of stories about the women who made them. *The Freedom Quilting Bee* shows a picture of China Grove Myles, one of the first known Pinecone quilters in the Wilcox County area. Callahan uses the name Cuckleburr in describing China's quilts and explains that Lucy Mingo, China's cousin by marriage, reported that China used really tiny triangles for her quilts, some as small as one inch. China and Lucy certainly knew each other's quilting styles and methods. Lucy made her squares larger, even though she learned to make the Pine Burr quilt from her Aunt China. Lucy's quilts were so wonderfully colorful and strong! Some of her quilts feature small pinecone blocks, set on point within a square block, which results in a secondary triangle pattern in the quilt.

Lucy Mingo with one of her Pine Burr quilts, now the state quilt of Alabama
Photo by Thea Storz

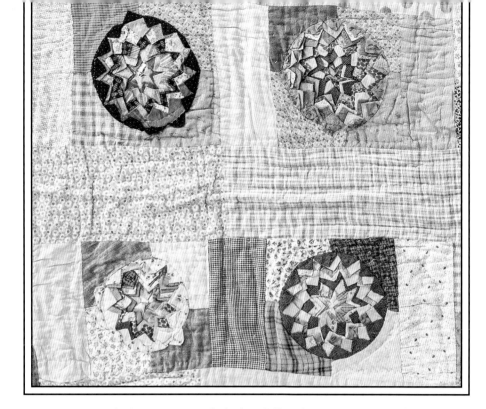

Detail of *Pine Burr 19 Blocks* (see full quilt image on page 55)

Mary W. Kerr dedicates an entire chapter to this style of quilting in *Southern Quilts*. In 1997, the Alabama legislature formally declared the Pine Burr quilt to be Alabama's official state quilt with the intent to honor the women who traditionally made these quilts, particularly the African American women associated with the Freedom Quilting Bee. The declaration acknowledged the Freedom Quilting Bee's relationship to the 1960s Civil Rights Movement and its national prominence as a rare Black women's cooperative.

Southern Quilts contains many excellent pictures, and I was excited to see several different variations of the technique. I also finally found a fine example of the large circular Pinecone quilt made the way Miss Sue taught me. It was said to be made by Rebecca Roscoe sometime around 1920. I was so excited to find this Pinecone quilt that after reading the book, I contacted the author, Mary Kerr, and sent her pictures of my own

Pinecone quilt work. She was delighted to see my quilts and invited me to show one of them at the Texas Quilt Museum for the exhibit *Southern Charm*, which she curated in June 2019. The quilt I displayed happened to be the first Pinecone quilt I made under Miss Sue's supervision.

It was amazing to me how each quilter in these books used the technique in a different way.

Some added just a little twist of their own, but others really branched out and used the same technique but in a completely different way. Another thing that struck me during that exhibit was how few people had seen a Pinecone quilt before. That realization, combined with my experience of how infrequently these quilts appeared in books and exhibits, made me begin to be concerned that this art would soon be lost.

A Brief History and Cultural Origins

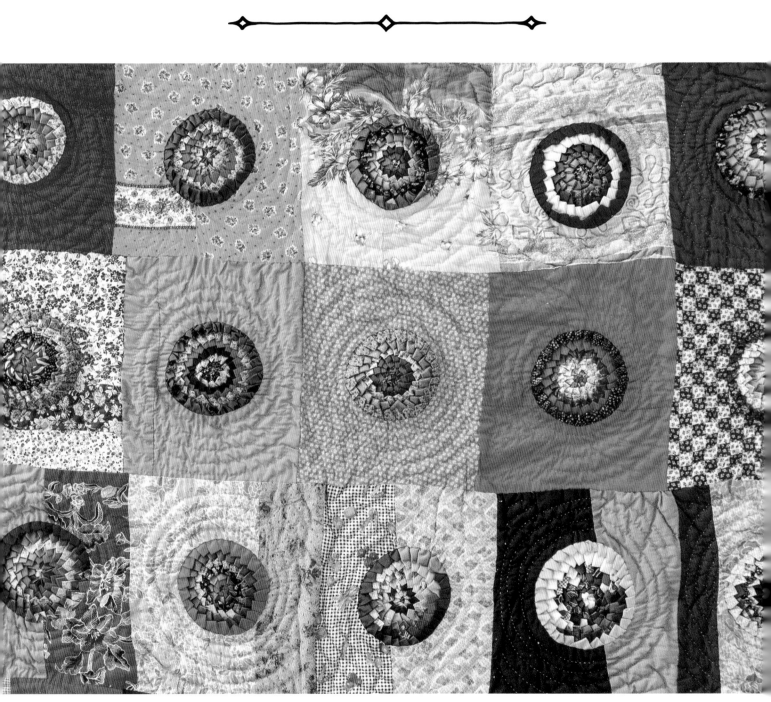

Detail of *30 Block Pine Burr* (see full quilt image on page 60)

Photo by Kenny Meza

Photo by White House Historical Association

In a 2015 interview between the then-first lady Michelle Obama and Jenna Bush, Mrs. Obama unveiled a painting that hung in the old family dining room of the White House. It was a painting by the artist Alma Woodsey Thomas. As soon as I saw it, I recognized the design. It was similar to the patterns used in my treasured Pinecone quilts. Right away, my curiosity was aroused. Her use of concentric circles, along with the way the undulating contrasts of light and dark gave spatial depth to her compositions, reminded me of my own quilting work. Could this be just coincidental? If not simply by chance, how prevalent was this sort of motif in the southeastern states and how far back might this tradition be found in African American decorative work?

Connections Across the South

Just as what I call a Pinecone quilt has other names that vary regionally, I have found that this specific pattern and style of quilting is also regional in another way. The geographic origins of the Pinecone quilts are within areas of the southern states. Within these states, there are regions that have common histories and similar social, political, and economic backgrounds. Although the people and communities in these regions are similarly situated and connected, they do have their own distinctive qualities and expressions.

As a collective landscape, this area was originally called the Black Belt region because of its fertile black soil, which was ideal for growing cotton. Most often when folks think of the Black Belt, they envision a group of places specifically in Alabama that are physically connected to each other. It is also common to identify the area for its heavy concentration of African American residents. While the Black Belt region of the United States does include seventeen Alabama counties—a strip that stretches from the east to west borders at the southern part of the state—they are actually part of a continuous swirl of regions that begins in east Texas. From there, the region stretches across parts of Arkansas, Louisiana, Tennessee, Mississippi, Alabama, Florida, and Georgia. The Black Belt then continues toward the north into parts of South Carolina, North Carolina, and Virginia.

After American Indian nations were removed from their native lands, this part of the South was eventually populated with numerous plantations—isolated rural landscapes that accommodated an economic system of plantocracy supported by the unpaid labor of enslaved Africans. From Reconstruction, through the days of low-wage sharecropping, and even to the present day, these rural counties have primarily remained geographically, racially, and culturally segregated.

The Pinecone in Gee's Bend

Family ties and community interdependencies within local society that were once necessary for survival influenced the design and making of quilts in Wilcox County, Alabama. Though some sources have credited China Grove Myles as the pioneer of the Pinecone quilt design, before her there were generations of quilters in her family. She grew up in an environment with many mentors around her. Her older sister, Rebecca Myles Jones, was also a very respected quilter in Gee's Bend. And while China taught Lucy Mingo, her niece by marriage, how to quilt using the Pine Burr technique, Lucy, too, had long ago learned how to quilt by watching and being taught by her grandmother and mother. In fact, she had four generations of quilters in her family. Back in those days, groups of women would go from house to house, taking turns helping each other make quilts. Lucy described their work as consisting of long, tiny rows sewn with a strong thread. She also emphasized to the author Nancy Callahan that China's work was made up of tiny pieces. Lucy Mingo's quilts are as fascinating as China's but very different. For the most part, Lucy works with large, colorful pieces that dominate the quilt, but she also uses a wider variety of sizes. Sometimes her skillful repetition of smaller, but not tiny, patches also dominates the composition because of her skillful placement and use of color.

Detail of *Vintage Pine Burr* (see full quilt image on page 54)
Similar to China Grove Myles's work, this antique quilt features 1″ triangles.
Photo by Kenny Meza

China was interviewed in an October 1975 *National Geographic* magazine article, "Alabama, Dixie to a Different Tune," and the national acclaim that followed brought in so many quilt requests from outside that some local women, including her sister Rebecca and niece Lucy, tried to help China keep up with the slew of orders. Although quiltmaking as a collective activity was traditional among earlier generations, those quilts of the past were made to be bed covers to keep families warm in winter. Long before the Freedom Quilting Bee was formed, working collectively had always been the culturally traditional way of quilting. But this business approach required unfamiliar ways and different kinds of decisions. There was already a push-and-pull relationship between the women who made the quilts in their own traditional styles and the retail market corporate clients up north who demanded specific standards. Discord in the relationship caused it to go bad, but the Pine Burr quilts remained popular. Although requests were ongoing, the team could not keep up with so many.

Nevertheless, the well-deserved popularity persevered. In 1997, 22 years after that *National Geographic* article, one of China Grove Myles's Pine Burr quilts was chosen to be the official state quilt of Alabama. The legislation specifically declared that it was a recognition of the women's work in Alabama's Black Belt region. A Gee's Bend Pine Burr quilt is now permanently associated with what is considered and celebrated as a distinctive representation of Alabama.

The Larger Southern Area

Approximately 200 miles southeast of Wilcox County, there is another part of the Black Belt that has significant connections to the unique Pinecone quilt, a region including four closely located towns. One is Bainbridge, in the southeastern corner of Georgia, and three—Marianna, Quincy, and Tallahassee—are in the Florida Panhandle, the northwestern section of the state. All four places are 40 miles or less apart from each other.

Miss Sue was born in Quincy, Florida, and moved to Bainbridge, Georgia, with her family at a very young age. Bainbridge is a small rural town just 26 miles from Tallahassee, where she also lived and did domestic work during part of her young adult life. She told me that all of her children had been born in Bainbridge, just 22 miles from her birthplace and childhood home of Quincy and 40 miles from Tallahassee. This vicinity has a concentration of places where quilters Arlene Dennis (Miss Sue) and Addie Bullock lived and worked.

Addie Bullock's 1966 quilt is the very first Pinecone quilt I found in my more formal research. It appeared in *Florida Quilts*, and the book indicates that Addie Bullock was originally from Sneads, Florida. Sneads is less than an hour away from both Quincy and Tallahassee, and I wonder if she and Miss Sue ever crossed paths, whether coincidentally or somehow intentionally, due to their mutual interest in quilting. They were both in the same regional, heavily Black community where people were still living under Jim

Crow laws. Segregation made the world they inhabited smaller because community places and amenities were more limited for them. In 1966, Miss Sue was in her mid-50s, and though she had a job, the everyday duties of her child-rearing days had passed. She might have been able to devote more time to quilting. Could a locally shared cultural style be something that influenced their common quilting style?

A Southern setting for a Southern quilt
You Are My Sunshine, 40″ × 40″, 2022, by Betty Ford-Smith
Project instructions for this quilt are available on page 90.

Other Artistic Expressions

Another interesting cross-connection possibility involves the artistry of Pinecone quilts and the artwork of Alma Woodsey Thomas. Alma's childhood hometown of Columbus, Georgia, was just ten miles across the Alabama border from Russell County, where her grandfather lived. She spent summers on his plantation farm. Alma was a curious, creative child. She loved being in that farm environment and held on to fond memories of it throughout her life. In 1952, when Alma Thomas was 62 years old, she used a photograph as reference to paint her grandfather's stately mansion, which is now in the collection of the Columbus Museum of Art. It wasn't until a bit later in life, when she was well into her 70s, that she started painting the abstract mosaics that became her signature. At the age of 16, she'd moved to Washington, D.C., with her family to escape the racism of the Deep South. Miss Sue was just 5 years old then and her family had already moved from Quincy, Florida, to Bainbridge, Georgia. The distance between Columbus and Bainbridge is 120 miles; from Russell County in Alabama to Bainbridge is 128 miles. There is a reasonably clear similarity between the artistic qualities of Alma's geometric mosaic paintings, particularly the bright concentric circles, and the quilts originating from this same region, such as the Pinecone quilt. As a child, might Alma Woodsey have come across this type of quilt in Columbus, Georgia, or Russell County in Alabama? Is it a possibility that in her later life, the period of her most prolific artwork, she may have recalled that aesthetic creative style by reflecting on a memory?

North Carolina Lumbee River Area

The northernmost area of the Black Belt in which I have found evidence of the Pinecone quilt is in southeastern North Carolina, where the Lumbee River is located. The area along the Lumbee River has been home territory for the Lumbee Tribe of North Carolina since the early 1700s. Although they have, to some degree, historically lived among and intermarried with African Americans in the region, the Lumbee Tribe is a distinct ethnic group. The pinecone symbol has historically been and still is, an essential symbol of Lumbee identity. The most spectacular Pinecone quilt I have ever come across was constructed by Maggie Lowrie Locklear, a socially affluent tribal woman, some 130 years ago. It is a truly remarkable work made up of 30,000 pieces. This quilt is on display at the Museum of the Southeast American Indian on the campus of the University of North Carolina at Pembroke. This clearly raises questions regarding the origins of the Pinecone quilt.

Pinecone Patchwork Quilt, 79″ × 55″, c. first half 20th century, hand pieced by Maggie Lowrie Locklear
Photo by the Museum of the Southeast American Indian

Pinecones are plentiful in the landscape along the Lumbee River and adjoining wetland regions. The Lumbee Pinecone, as the symbol is called, gets its name from the longleaf variety of pines. It adorns traditional ceremonial garments, traditional jewelry and, more recently, appears on contemporary fashion jewelry, T-shirts, and souvenir items. Nevertheless, it has been and still is a long-standing symbol of Lumbee cultural identity and customs. In many representations of their traditional ways of life, and as is common with Native American nations, the Lumbee people adapted well to living in and using the resources of the natural environment.

Perhaps the Lumbee taught this quilting method to others living in the same area and it spread that way? It is implausible that two groups of people lived so closely together and didn't share anything.

African Connections

Pinecone quilts have a particularly interesting resemblance to some West African aesthetics. Concentric circles formed by the arrangement of triangles within round bands that radiate from a common center create a rhythmic pattern. In some cases, the layout aligns the triangles so that meet at each other's base end, which then creates the boundary between two concentric rings. An example can be seen in the Bamileke Elephant Mask from Cameroon.

Elephant Mask from Cameron Bamileke people, Village of Banjoun,
c. 1910–1930, Dallas Museum of Art
Photo by Mary Harrsch,—Own work, CC BY-SA 4.0, https://commons.wikimedia.org/w/index.php?curid=95579453

Photo by demidoff / Shutterstock.com

Other arrangements also show triangles consecutively placed next to each other, but with each triangle in each band facing the same direction. The round Bwa Owl Mask from Burkina Faso exhibits this pattern. Both design looks are exciting. Whether brightly colorful or with palettes of indigo and neutral earth tones, they make for dynamic compositions. In that way, Pinecone quilts are similar.

Photo by Erika Alatalo

Some dwellings in the villages of the Kassena tribe in Burkina Faso are decorated with intense geometric patterns of triangles by the women of the villages, much like the traditional quilting that was done by groups of women in Gee's Bend. The geometric patterns are reminiscent of pinecones, but they are not the same. Some of the buildings are round, and the conical thatch roofs that sit atop the circular walls have a center-pointed tip with a small circle from which everything radiates out, similar to a pinecone. However, the round building walls are flat and there is no texture like pinecones have, which makes a big difference.

Robert Farris Thompson, a renowned art historian, and anthropologist, did extensive studies of African influence and presence in the Western world. He showed direct (not theoretical) connections and likenesses in spiritual symbols and many secular elements of culture and environments that rely on a cultural geography way of understanding. In my own spaces and my experiences as a retailer and collector of African artifacts, I also saw similarities that prompted me to think about origins. Thompson ties the invisible to the visible and vice versa in clear ways. I can see that some things about African art have a certain *spirit* that seems comparable to the visual dynamics I can see in my Pinecone quilts. I also realize some things came from Africa through memories, then were passed down through generations. Black music is an example of that: No one brought drums or musical scores with them, but jazz and gospel music exist here in the United States.

Many respected scholars of African art and culture have compared quilt artistry to West African design styles. In "Material Truths: The Quilts of Gee's Bend at the Whitney Museum of Art, An Exhibition Review," cultural historian and curator Michael J.

Prokopow makes several references to African aesthetics in his discussion of the African American quilts on display. He compares the design qualities of the Gee's Bend quilts to the cloth traditions of Kobe and Asante cultures. In her introduction to *The Quilts of Gee's Bend*, Alvia Wardlaw, a noted art scholar and expert on African American quilts, discusses how Gee's bend women, living in collective isolation for generations, certainly shared creative inspiration with each other and how it would be reasonable to assume that traditions were passed down through many generations. However, traditions change out of necessity and opportunity. Traditional design approaches are met with new fabrics, and people are exposed to other ideas and traditions outside of their immediate communities and region. All of these things had impacts, as did the availability of technology.

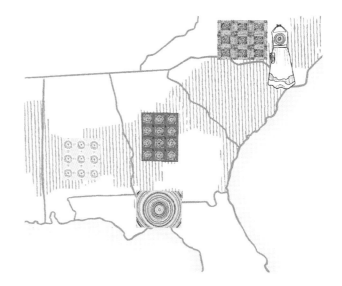

On the other hand, Cuesta Benberry, who wrote *A Piece of My Soul: Quilts by Black Arkansans*, the first book I read on African American quilts, took the position that African Americans drew inspiration from what they saw around them, whatever was popular in the mainstream, not retained African traditions. She commented that the Pinecone quilt was not exclusively African American, but it was considered very special by the Black quilters who continued to make Pinecone quilts long after they were no longer commercially popular. The women who continued to make them created their own design variations that took on clearly different looks as they evolved.

The exact origins are unclear, but it is clear that this technique is unique to the South, and especially the Southeast United States. The women living in close proximity to one another clearly shared this technique with each other and then passed it down through generations.

As I found that so few people now knew about Pinecone, Pine Burr, or Cuckleburr quilts and that my own efforts to learn more about these remarkable quilts was not easy, I began to worry that these skills were now disappearing. Through my research experience, seeing similar motifs in other places and other artwork and learning more about the women who made these quilts and handed down their skills from generation to generation was truly inspiring. In fact, it inspired me to get back into education, this time teaching anyone willing to learn how to make Pinecone quilts the way Miss Sue taught me. In the following chapters, you'll learn how to make your own Pinecone quilt and quilt projects. This special technique and history won't be lost.

Sharing the
Tradition

◇————◇————◇

The first Pinecone quilt I made under Miss Sue's supervision was featured that same year in the local paper, the *News Sun*, on February 25, 2005.

The thought of where this craft could take me never entered my mind, I just wanted to make Miss Sue known locally for her quilts.

I hadn't considered entering any quilt shows, but my first general quilting instructor, Joan, encouraged me to get a feel for what quilters and the public thought of this type of quilting. I arrived at the 40th annual Lake Placid Arts and Crafts Country Fair with my quilt. When I presented my quilt, I was told that it did not qualify for the exhibit because it was technically not a quilt. Quilts had to have the traditional three layers: a top, a middle layer of batting, and a bottom layer. One of the officials walked up and told the ladies at the registration desk that my quilt was something different and people should be given a chance to see it. As soon as it was hung, people reacted with amazement to the colors, the little folded fabric pieces, the amount of fabric used, the large size, and the fact that it was all hand sewn. None of them had ever seen a quilt like this, and that made me want to share these quilts more widely. I displayed my quilts in a second show, and I began to start feeling comfortable speaking publicly about quilts.

When a friend asked me to teach her how to make a Pinecone quilt, I realized that five years had passed since I had picked up a needle

My quilts on exhibit at the International Quilt Museum in Lincoln, Nebraska
Photo by Camilo Sanchez

to start a new quilt and I was beginning to forget how. Teaching someone else seemed the perfect way to jump back in. I began teaching the same way Miss Sue taught me, but I quickly realized that starting with a king-size sheet didn't work for everyone. It was frustrating and overwhelming and my first student gave up after one lesson. I completed the quilt my student had begun. I was feeling as though there was a hole in my retired life, so I chose green to symbolize growth, health, new beginnings, money, nature, environment, and energy. It turned out to be the unexpectedly beautiful *Green Pinecone Quilt* (page 62). As successfully as it turned out, completing this quilt was more difficult than I'd hoped it would be. I had to quilt it without Miss Sue's supervision and advice and all her dos and don'ts were no longer fresh in my head.

I kept working and completed my third Pinecone quilt in 2014, which was accepted into an exhibition at the Alice and William Jenkins Gallery at the Crealdé School of Art. I was honored to meet two Gee's Bend quilters that were also part of the exhibition. After that, the inspiration for another quilt came swiftly. Katell Renon, an online friend and French blogger, wrote about my green Pinecone quilt. She'd also posted about her love for the book *The Color Purple*. I was so excited she was blogging about my work that I decided to make a quilt in her honor, and I named it *Purple Katell* (page 61).

Though I was really enjoying exhibiting my quilts, my true hope was to teach and pass the tradition on. After a couple of failed teaching experiments, the local community college, South Florida State College (SFSC) in Avon Park asked me to teach Pine Cone quilting as a community education class. This time I decided to provide each student a small block of fabric 24˝ × 24˝ so it wasn't so overwhelming. Finally, I'd found my path. To this day, I don't know why I believed everyone had the patience to learn by sitting for long hours sewing triangles to a king-size sheet.

In 2018, Megan Stepe became my apprentice through the Florida Division of Historical Resources Folklife Apprenticeship Program. Though Megan is a young person with a busy work and social life, she completed a 40˝ × 40˝ quilt, and we gave demonstrations and displayed our quilts at that year's Florida Folk Festival in White Springs, Florida. Megan created an amazing Pinecone quilt made with all the old fabric she could find in her house including old childhood pajamas, costumes, pillowcases, tablecloths, scarves, dresses, shorts, and pants. The finished quilt looks like an antique and reminds her of what she was doing when each piece of cloth was in use and where it came from in her life. Using old fabrics is great because they are often easier to sew and they bring back memories. Megan is now a college art professor and museum curator and continues to help carry on the Pinecone technique.

My apprentice, Megan Stepe, helps to keep the Pinecone tradition alive

I began to get more attention and was now traveling to keep the tradition alive. I've since participated in numerous art and folk festivals. It is hard to be away from home for three to five days at a time, and it is tiring to do all that's involved: driving long distances; setting up and breaking down tables, chairs, and sometimes even tents; and packing and moving heavy quilts. It can be exhausting to sit and engage with many people for days at a time, but it is also exciting to meet so many people and see them engage with my quilts, learn to make them, and want to learn more.

Sometimes I think I need to start lifting weights to build up the strength needed to continue traveling, dragging suitcases, and holding up these heavy quilts. I continue to keep pushing myself because I remember that Miss Sue, at 98, could still sit on the floor to pin and cut fabric and then get up like a spring chicken. And at the end of the day, it feels really great to know someone loved your work, is interested in what you are doing, and wants to exchange stories. It also feels good to know that, among quilters, it does not make any difference where you come from, or what nationality, race, or religion you are.

Festivals aren't always easy but they are always rewarding

At the same time as I was traveling to festivals, my quilts began to be included in museum exhibits. The first time my quilts were shown was in 2016 at the SFSC Museum of Florida Art and Culture in Avon Park. Though I was nervous and anxious about how well the quilts might be received, the exhibit went well and, as a result, interest in Pinecone quilts grew. My second museum experience was in Tallahassee, Florida, at the

Museum of Florida History. Two of my quilts were scheduled to be in the show, but after driving five hours to deliver the quilts, I was told that they could not be shown because they lacked sleeves and were not ready for hanging. Though my quilts had been shown before, I'd never heard of hanging sleeves and I almost cried. Then a woman came up to me and said she would take them to her house and put the sleeves on for me. This angel,

Jeanne Brenner, rescued me, but neither of us knew what she was getting into by offering to add sleeves to 28-pound quilts! It took Jeanne five days to add the sleeves. I drove back to Tallahassee for the ribbon cutting ceremony on opening night, and my husband and I stood in the lobby with Jeanne and her husband and waited anxiously for the doors to open so we could see all the quilts. It was such an honor to be among so many experienced and talented quilters. I started to tear up because I could not believe that so many people appreciated the hard work that went into completing these quilts and because they would never have seen them if not for the kindness of a stranger.

From Florida to France, 24″ × 24″, 2017, hand pieced by Betty Ford-Smith
I made this piece as a gift to my friend Katell. Each fabric was selected intentionally
to be symbolic of an aspect of our friendship.

Katell continued to blog about my work and continues to be one of my strongest supporters, a source of inspiration, and a friend. She arranged for me to travel to France to give workshops, and my husband and I were able to add a few days in Paris to our trip for a long overdue vacation. While teaching a local class, one of the students offered to connect me with a friend who had been living in France for years. Her friend met up with us and spent three days showing us the real Paris. My workshop attendees were very receptive and

Presenting a lecture on my quilts at The National Quilt Museum in Paducah, Kentucky
Photo by National Quilt Museum, Paducah, KY

l loved seeing all their beautiful quilts and handwork. In fact, some of the women could do work so small that I was presented with a Pinecone pin only three and a half inches in diameter. I am still trying to make one that small. At the end of the trip, I came back with a bag full of gifts from generous quilters and friends that I will remember for the rest of my life. Again, I want to reiterate the kindness and generosity of quilters I have encountered everywhere, including quilters I've only ever called or emailed. Quilters are the most generous group of people I know.

In 2019, I was contacted by the National Quilt Museum about exhibiting my quilts. My husband and I went to Paducah, Kentucky, for the opening exhibit during what turned out to be the coldest weather on record for the first week of February. When we arrived, the airport had shut down and taxis had stopped running. A passenger from our flight asked where we were going and offered to take us to our hotel. Another wonderful stranger to the rescue!

I was also honored to be chosen to participate in the National Quilt Museum's Block of the Month Club, a group of more than 13,000 quilters nationwide who learn new quilting techniques by copying the block or quilt design of the month. I was so pleased to have so many quilters learning to carry on this tradition. Since making the block of the month for the National Quilt Museum in Kentucky, thousands of quilters have now been exposed to the Pinecone, or Cuckleburr, quilt.

Back in 2004, sitting with Miss Sue in front of her decorated fireplace, I never imagined that this art form would take me on such an amazing journey or spur me to pass down this unique quilting technique to so many, ensuring that the art form won't be lost. After the National Quilt Museum exhibit, I began to receive commissions for quilts and requests for classes, workshops, and lectures, ensuring that I can continue to teach more people and encourage them to pass down the tradition. My only problem now is that there is not enough time in the day.

Sharing Miss Sue's technique with patrons of
The National Quilt Museum in Paducah, Kentucky

Photo by National Quilt Museum, Paducah, KY

Gallery of Vintage and Contemporary Pinecone Quilts

Although best efforts have been made to provide dates of completion
for the vintage quilts in this chapter, many of the dates are estimates.
Estimated dates are indicated by an approximate decade or range of decades.

Vintage Brown Circular Pine Burr, 13½″ diameter, c. 1920–1949, unknown maker
This was completely handmade; notice that the triangles are narrower than most.

Pine Burr Quilt Doily, 12½″ diameter, c. 1930s, unknown maker
Made of feed sacks from the 1930s, this piece is completely handmade, also with narrower triangles.

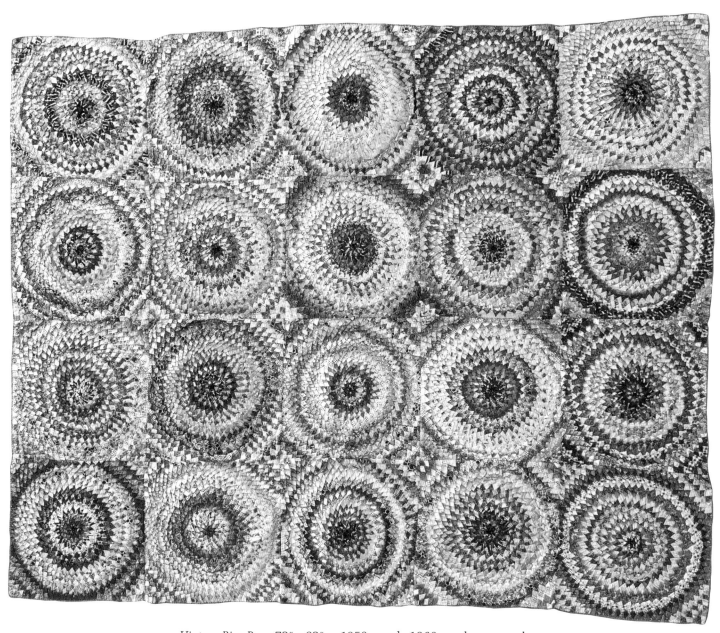

Vintage Pine Burr, 73″ × 82″, c. 1950s–early 1960s, unknown maker
Rare vintage Pine Burr quilt created using 1″ triangles, purchased 2017
Photo by Kenny Meza

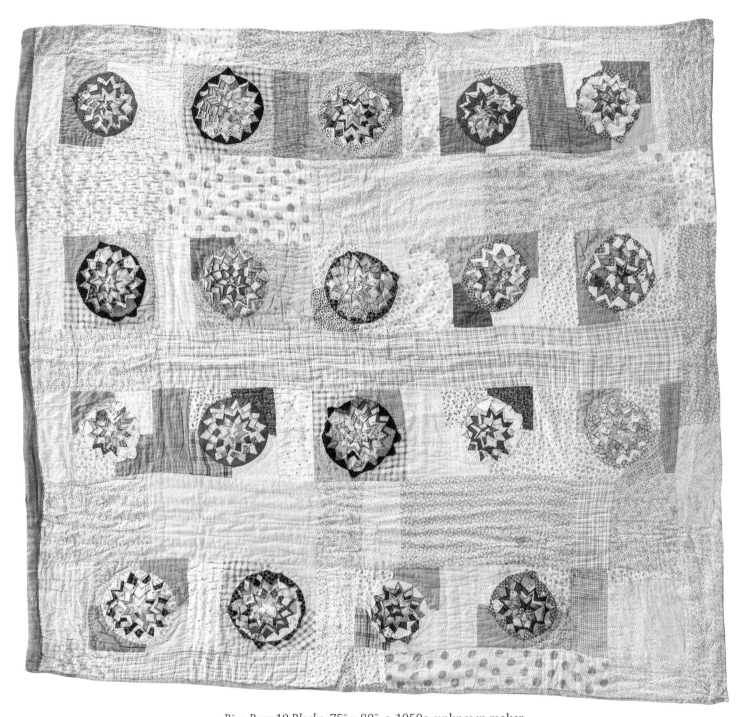

Pine Burr 19 Blocks, 75˝ × 80˝, c. 1950s, unknown maker
Notice that one block is missing. This is likely intentional, done as a deliberate mistake
to "fool the devil," a common superstition.
Photo by Kenny Meza

Antique Pine Burr Quilt with Blue Sashing, 82″ × 65″, c. 1950–1960, unknown maker
Photo by Kenny Meza

◇ ◇

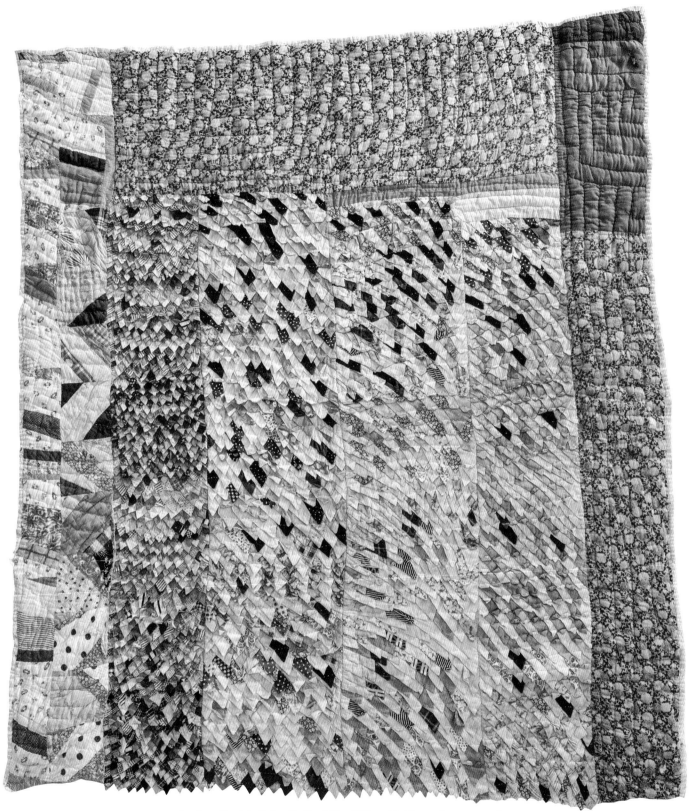

Antique Prairie Point Quilt, 68″ × 75″, c. 1940s, unknown maker

Photo by Kenny Meza

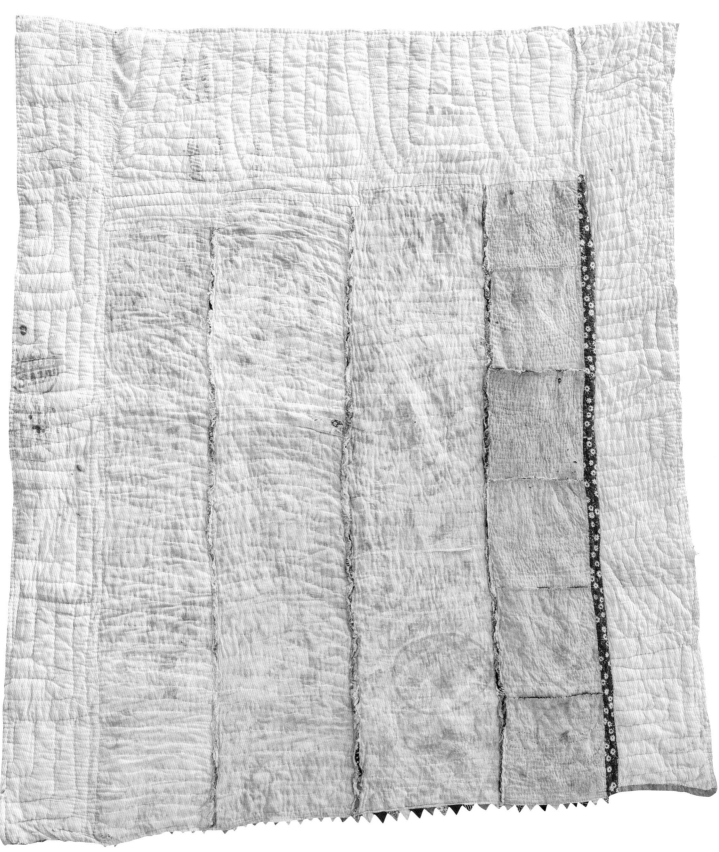

Back of *Antique Prairie Point Quilt* (see full quilt on page 57)
The back is pieced using sugar and salt sacks.

Domino

Cane Sugar

Domino

Cane Sugars

The perfect sugar for coffee and tea. In 2 pound cartons

In 5 and 6 pound cartons too as 10 and 25 pound cotton bags

merican Sugar

ning Company

New York, N.Y.

American Sugar

Refining Company

New York, N.Y.

Detail of *Antique Prairie Point Quilt* (see full quilt on page 57)

30 Block Pine Burr, 86″ × 104″, c. 1980–2000, unknown maker
Found at an estate sale in Greenwood, South Carolina

Photo by Kenny Meza

Purple Katell, 99″ × 66″, 2014, hand pieced by Betty Ford-Smith
The completed quilt weighs 29 pounds.

Green Pinecone Quilt, 100″ × 82″, 2014, hand pieced by Betty Ford-Smith
The completed quilt weighs 28 pounds.

Eye of the Storm, 62˝ × 112˝, c. 1990s, hand pieced by Arlene Dennis
Photo by Betty Ford-Smith

Betty and Butler Cuckleburr Quilt, 80″ × 80″, 2017, designed by Butler Henry Smith Jr.
and hand pieced by Betty Ford-Smith
This quilt took six months to complete, uses 5″ fabric squares, and weighs 28 pounds.

Detail of *Betty and Butler Cuckleburr Quilt* (see full quilt on page 64)
This quilt was made under the watchful eyes of my husband. He selected all the fabrics, and I did all the cutting
and hand sewing. Twenty two-dollar bills, which we received at our wedding, are placed in folded triangles
throughout this quilt for prosperity and memories.

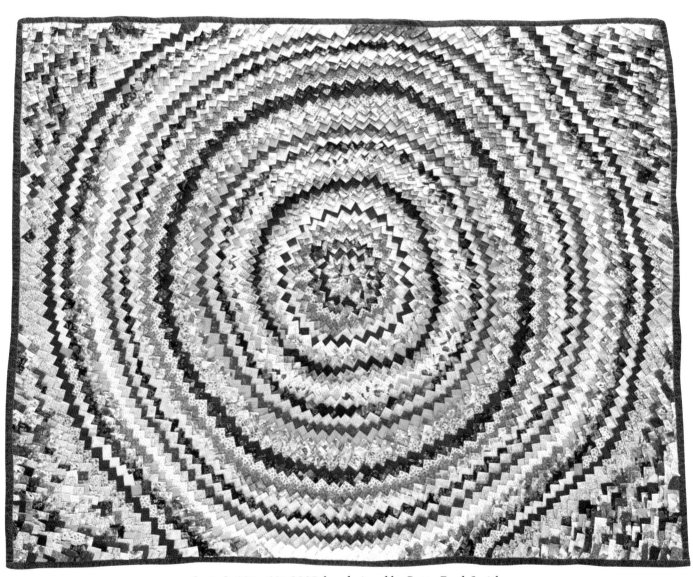

Susie Q, 80″ × 68″, 2005, hand pieced by Betty Ford-Smith
The first quilt I made with Miss Sue. This quilt only weighs 17 pounds
because it primarily uses lighter garment fabrics, which weigh less than quilting cottons.

Detail of *Susie Q* (see full quilt on page 66)
The corner of my first Pinecone quilt—looking closely, you can see that
this uses mostly older washed and worn fabrics.

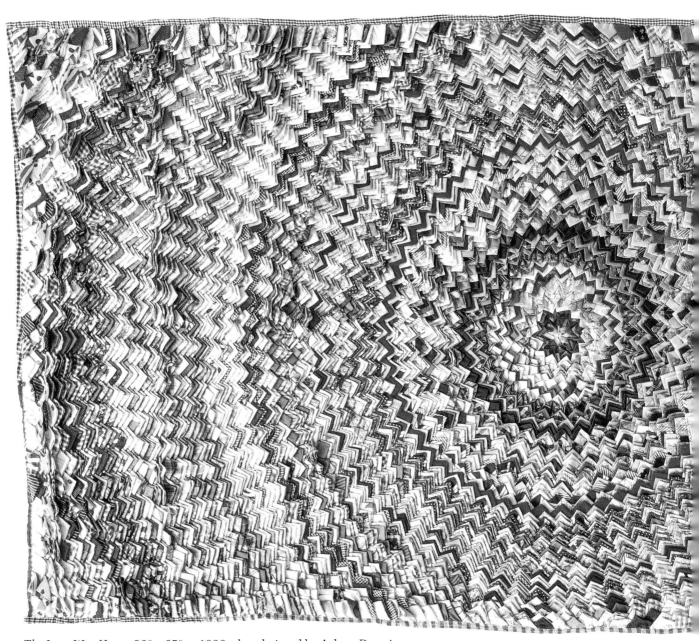

The Long Way Home, 90″ × 65″, c. 1990s, hand pieced by Arlene Dennis
Photo by Kenny Meza

Detail of *The Long Way Home*

The Healing Quilt, 23½˝ × 23½˝, 2017, hand pieced by Betty Ford-Smith
This quilt, in particular, seems to change color depending on the light and the surrounding colors.

Little Pink Victorian Garden, 15½″ × 15½″, 2016, hand pieced by Betty Ford-Smith

Caribbean Dream, 61″ × 63″, 2018, hand pieced by Betty Ford-Smith
This finished quilt weighs only 19 pounds because lighter and used fabrics were included.

Toulouse, 81″ × 84″, 2018, hand pieced by Betty Ford-Smith
This quilt weighs 28 pounds. I started this quilt as a demonstration piece for the Florida Folk Festival, but completed it for the National Quilt Museum in Paducah, Kentucky. I dedicated it to my French friends after returning from a teaching trip to France.

Midnight Stars, 17½″ × 18½″, 2017, hand pieced by Betty Ford-Smith
The stars on the dark blue fabric glow in the dark.

Photo by Anthony Pasquino

Veronica Ann, 38″ × 40″, 2019, hand pieced by Betty Ford-Smith
For this baby quilt, I incorporated used fabrics and spaced the rows of triangles further apart,
making a much lighter quilt, weighing just seven pounds.

Eternity, 8˝ × 8˝, 2017, hand pieced by Betty Ford-Smith
This small piece is displayed in a white shadow box.

Folk Festival, 22″ × 22″, 2016, hand pieced by Betty Ford-Smith
I carefully lined up each row of triangles to mirror the row before, creating a zigzag effect.

Make Your Own Pinecone Quilt

<hr />

Making Pinecone quilts is simple enough, but it takes a bit of practice to get the hang of it. In this chapter, I'll explain the tools and fabrics you'll need and walk you through the process by making a sample. You can read through to learn the method, but if you want to follow along, I'll provide the fabric amounts so that you can work alongside me to learn the method.

Tools

To get started, you will need some basic tools. Pinecone quilting has been handed down for generations, so you do not need anything fancy!

- Standard 12″ ruler

- Fabric shears (I prefer spring-action ergonomic scissors.)

- Embroidery scissors

- Doll needle, 3″ or 3½″

- #10 crochet thread

- Safety pins

- Pencil

- Straight pins

- Cardboard, template plastic, or scrap fabric 5″ × 5″ to use as a template

- Needle-nose pliers (optional)

- Needle threader (optional)

◇ *Helpful Hints*

- You'll be doing a lot of cutting. I highly recommend ergonomic spring-action scissors (the ones that look like a gardening tool).

- A needle threader is useful when your eyes become tired.

- Needle-nose pliers are helpful when it is hard to pull the needle through tougher fabrics.

ALTERNATIVE THREADS

This book teaches the Pinecone quilt technique just as I learned it from Miss Sue and just as Miss Sue's grandmother taught it to her. Using the traditional crochet thread to stitch all the layers together can, admittedly, be a challenge. However, the results are stunning, the quilts will last, and they stay true to this folk art tradition. Additionally, crochet thread is all cotton, which is undoubtedly why it was the choice of earlier generations—it is what would have been on hand. However, if you have trouble getting the crochet thread through the fabric layers and are about to give up, don't. There are alternatives. If you need to try something different, try using button and carpet, upholstery, or outdoor thread. All of these options are strong and easier to stitch.

Fabrics

Before you begin, you will need fabrics for the quilt base, the sewn triangles, and the binding.

For the base or foundation fabric, choose a single piece of fabric that is soft to the touch. It should be thin enough that it will be easy to sew through multiple layers of fabric, but sturdy enough to not tear once all the pieces are added. Miss Sue used an old bedsheet for most of her quilts. Keep in mind that the larger the quilt you make, the heavier it will be when finished, so choose a sturdier fabric for larger pieces. For this technique demonstration, you will need ⅜ yard of lightweight cotton fabric for the base.

For the triangle points, collect assorted cotton fabric scraps or yardage. Gather a variety of fabrics, including a few solids and smaller allover busy prints such as florals, paisleys, plaids, polka dots, stripes, stars, or animal prints. Busier fabrics blend better and hide the occasional stitch that peeks through. Batik fabrics are not recommended as they are hard to hand sew. For this technique demonstration, you will need approximately 3¼ yards of a variety of prints and solids (150–175 squares 5″ × 5″ for a 12″ × 12″ block). Even though only 3¼ yards is needed to complete the sample piece, I always gather much more fabric than I think I will need to ensure I have a variety of prints and colors and that I don't run out of one and have to head back to the fabric store.

◇ Helpful Hints

Used and worn fabrics can actually be much easier to work with than newer, stiffer fabric. Consider skipping a trip to the fabric store and instead rummaging through your old clothing and any used household cloth items that are ready for donation. Thrift stores are also a great source for used fabrics.

The following chart provides estimates of how many yards of fabric you might need to complete a quilt. These estimates are based on my typical spacing, using 5″ squares of fabric to create the triangles. Keep in mind that these are estimates only. If you space your triangles more closely or use smaller squares of fabric, you will need more yardage.

Fabric Amounts for Standard Quilt Sizes

Quilt	Size	Yards
Lap	48″ × 48″	17–19
Throw	60″ × 60	25–27
Twin	60″ × 90″	40–42
Double	80″ × 90″	53–55

Audition different fabrics for the binding. Dark fabrics will frame the piece, coordinating fabrics will disappear, and contrasting fabrics can add a pop of color. For Pinecone quilts finished as a square or rectangle, binding cut on the grain is the way to go. The binding strips will usually be 3¼″ wide and 3″ longer than each side of the piece. For the technique example, you will need ¼ yard or one fat quarter of fabric.

◇ *Helpful Hints*

- Select all your fabrics before you begin.

- Choose fabrics with bold prints; solid fabrics tend to show the stitches more.

- Avoid batiks; they are very hard to sew by hand.

Basic Technique

1. Cut 1 square 12″ × 12 of the base fabric. To find the center, take one corner and fold the square over into a triangle and then fold it again, corner to corner, to make a smaller triangle.

2. Place a small safety pin at the top fold of the triangle to mark the center of the base cloth. Unfold the base square.

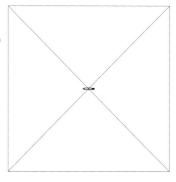

3. From cardboard, template plastic, or scrap fabric, make a 5″ × 5″ template. Use the template to cut 4 squares 5″ × 5″ from the triangle fabrics for the center.

4. Take one of the squares you just cut and fold it into a triangle twice, just like you did for the base fabric. Finger-press the triangle. Place the triangle onto the base fabric with the tip of the triangle touching the safety pin in the center. Pin.

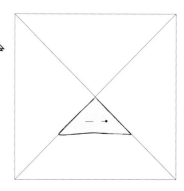

5. Fold another 5″ × 5″ square into a triangle, finger-press it, and place it in the center just above the first triangle with the point touching

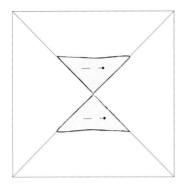

the safety pin. Be sure the opening of each triangle (the double-folded side) is facing the same direction, moving clockwise or counterclockwise. Pin.

6. Fold and finger-press another 5″ × 5″ square and pin it down with the point touching the safety pin. Repeat the same process with the

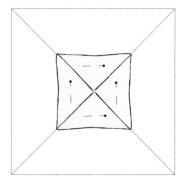

fourth and final center triangle, again being sure that the folded sides are facing the same direction.

---

7. Thread the needle with a single length of crochet thread and tie a double knot at the end. Begin stitching with the knot on top of

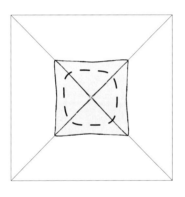

the triangles. Using a running stitch, sew a circle about 1½″ from the center to keep the triangles from moving. Three to four stitches per triangle will be sufficient. Remove the pins and the safety pin, but do not cut the thread.

◇ *Helpful Hints*

- When folding the fabric triangles, I finger-press each piece, but some quilters like to use an iron.

- After the second or third row, put away the pins and place each triangle piece one at a time.

- Double-knot all the thread ends and only cut the thread when you need to rethread the needle.

8. Cut 6 squares 5″ × 5″ of a contrasting color for the second row. Depending on how much you overlap, you may need up to 7 or 8 pieces. Fold

and finger-press each square into a triangle, as you did for the first layer. Add the second layer of triangles on top of the first layer, leaving a small gap in the center so the first layer can still be seen. Overlap each triangle in the second layer a little and try to form a star shape in the center. Pin the triangles in place.

◇ *Helpful Hints*

- As you work, keep checking to be sure the stitches from the previous layer are not showing from the front. However, keep in mind that this is folk art, have fun, and don't sweat the details—there will always be a few stitches that show.

- Keep all the knots on top of the piece. Knots nested between the fabric triangle layers are less likely to come apart.

9. Bring the needle to the top of the piece by stitching up from the first layer to the top of the second layer. Using a running stitch in a circular pattern, sew the second row down. Stitch through all layers of fabric so the stitches are visible on the back of the piece. Remove the pins but do not cut the thread.

10. Select fabric of a different color for the third row and cut 7–10 squares 5″ × 5″. Fold and finger-press each square into a triangle.

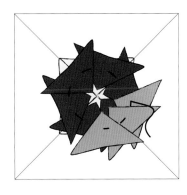

Place these triangles on top of the second layer, leaving a small part of the second-layer triangles visible. Each triangle in the new layer should overlap the last triangle you added. Keep the points positioned toward the center, and pin down and sew this third layer as you did the first two layers. Stitch through all layers of fabric so the stitches are visible on the back of the piece. When you reach the end of the piece of thread, tie it off with a double knot and begin stitching with a new piece of thread. Keep all the knots on top of the piece.

◇ *Helpful Hints*

• I like to precut at least 30–40 squares of various fabrics because once I get started, I do not want to lose the rhythm or the fabric pattern.

• Keep in mind that each person spaces the triangles differently, making every finished quilt unique. It is difficult to determine how many pieces are needed for each layer, but you will soon get a feel for your spacing and how many additional triangles you need for each successive layer.

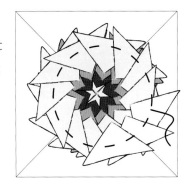

11. For the fourth and all subsequent layers, you need at least 30 squares in various fabrics ready at a time because once you get started, you will not want to lose the rhythm or the fabric pattern. For my example, I chose a contrasting color for each layer.

12. For each layer, fold, finger-press, and add the triangles one at a time, always going in the same direction in a circular pattern. Each piece should overlap the previous triangle. Stitch each triangle down one at a time, remembering to stitch through all layers of fabric. No pinning is necessary after the third layer.

◇ *Helpful Hints*

• The positioning of each triangle is very important—take your time.

• Don't be afraid to take a row out and start again.

• Don't give up! These quilts take time but are well worth the effort.

13. Keep sewing until you get to the edges, the circle is complete, and the final full circle of triangles overlaps the edges of the base fabric. Stitch these last layers on carefully, being sure that all of the stitches go through the triangles and the base layer of fabric.

14. Turn the block over to make sure the pieces fully cover the base fabric. It is now time to cover the corners of the base fabric.

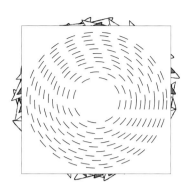

15. One layer at a time and continuing the circular pattern, sew layers of triangles onto each corner until

the tip is covered. Complete one corner at a time, and continue adding pieces until you get to the edge of the fabric. Check to make sure you are still sewing on the base fabric. Each corner may be a little different depending on how much of the base fabric was left showing.

16. Flip the piece over and make sure that no stitches have missed the base layer. If there are stitches that have missed the base layer, tack them down from the top to secure the layer of triangles. Being sure not to clip any of the threads,

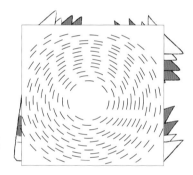

slowly and carefully trim the extra fabric hanging over the edge of the base fabric before you put the binding around the quilt.

◆ *Helpful Hints*

• Before you trim, check carefully for any stitches that missed the base fabric layer. If you cut any stitches as you trim the piece for binding, you could cut threads that could allow some of the triangles to fall off. Trim slowly and carefully!

• Do not use the sewing machine to sew on the binding. After all of your hard work, take the time to add that final handmade touch.

• Pinecone quilts don't always end up perfectly square. The number of fabric layers in any one area of the quilt varies, making some areas bulkier than others, which can result in some edges having a slight curve. Remember, this is folk art!

Binding

1. Cut the binding strips. For this sample piece, you will need 4 strips 3¼″ × 15″. Each strip will need to be long enough to overlap the end of each side of the base fabric by 1½″.

2. Start by pinning one binding strip right side down to the back of the base fabric, lining up one long end of the binding strip with one side of the base. Pin the binding 1″ from the edge and stitch the binding to the back of the block using a running stitch, stitching through the base fabric and 1–2 additional layers of fabric and keeping the seam 1″ from the edge.

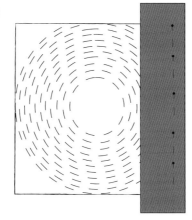

3. Fold over the binding strip along the line you just stitched and flip the piece over. Fold the long edge of the binding strip over approximately

¼″ and pin the binding to the front of the piece, making sure you have covered the final stitches. Whipstitch the binding to the front of the piece.

---

4. Repeat on the remaining 3 sides.

5. Tuck the excess binding inside at each corner (just like you would if you were turning a sock) and whipstitch closed.

---

6. Your Pinecone quilt block is complete once the binding is on all four sides.

Pinecone Projects to Get You Started

◆━━━━◆━━━━◆

Sometimes it is hard to know where to start. It's easy to fall in love with these quilts, only to realize that you only have so much space to show them off. Never fear—in this chapter, I offer a variety of projects, from a diminutive corsage to an intricate multiblock quilt, to give you plenty of places to start and inspiration for how to show off your stunning creations.

Puffy Pinecone Pillow

FINISHED PILLOW: 20″ × 20″

This Puffy Pinecone Pillow is the perfect project to get you started. It's small enough that you can always see the finish line, and if you add the pillow back, you can instantly show off your very own piece of folk art. If you want an even easier-to-finish project, I will walk you through how to frame your finished piece in a shadow box and skip the extra sewing.

MATERIALS

Yardages are based on fabric 40″ wide.

Base fabric: ⅓ yard muslin

Backing: ¾ yard

Triangle points: 5–6 yards assorted red and pink prints (18–20 different prints are ideal)

Binding: ½ yard

#10 crochet thread

Doll sewing needle

Sewing thread

Hand sewing needle

18″ × 18″ pillow insert

Optional: Shadow box, 20″ × 20″

CUTTING

Base Fabric

Cut 1 piece of muslin 20″ × 20″ for the base.

Pillow Backing Fabric

Cut 2 pieces 15″ × 20″ for the pillow backing.

Triangle Points

Cut 4 squares 5″ × 5″ for the center layer.

Cut 6 squares 5″ × 5″ for the second layer.

Cut 8 squares 5″ × 5″ for the third layer.

Cut 2–10 additional squares 5″ × 5″ per layer for each subsequent layer.

Binding Fabric

Cut 4 strips 3¼″ × 23″.

Construction

1. Following the Basic Technique instructions (page 81), create a 20″ × 20″ pinecone block.

2. On each pillow backing piece, fold over one long end ½″ and press. Fold over again ½″ and press. Topstitch across the folded edge.

3. Align one piece of pillow backing to the top of your pinecone piece with the sewn edge toward the center of the piece and pin. Align the other pillow backing piece along the bottom of the pinecone piece with the sewn edge overlapping the other pillow backing piece and pin.

4. Following the Binding instructions (page 84), add binding to finish your pillowcase.

SHADOW BOX
WALL HANGING VARIATION

Following the Basic Technique instructions (page 81),
create a 20˝ × 20˝ pinecone block. Follow the Binding instructions (page 84)
to finish the piece. Carefully place the finished piece in the shadow box.

Pinecone Baby Quilt

FINISHED QUILT: 40˝ × 40˝

The classic song *You Are My Sunshine* was my inspiration for this bright and cheerful baby-sized quilt. Because of the weight of the finished quilt, it is not intended for use in a crib or on the baby. It is for decorative use or for some fun and tactile tummy-time play on the floor. The sunny yellow background will light up any nursery and the high contrast layers of color add a sense of movement and merriment. Choosing a coordinating fabric for the binding makes the illusion of movement continue off the quilt top.

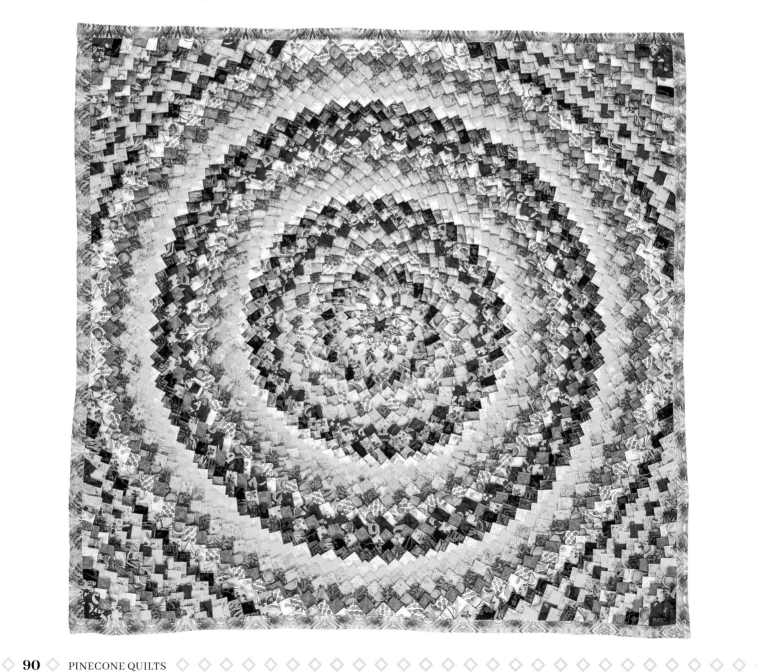

MATERIALS

Yardages are based on fabric 40˝ wide.

Base fabric: 1¼ yards lightweight cotton or muslin

Binding: ¾ yard coordinating fabric

Triangle points: 13–15 yards assorted yellow and contrasting prints and solids (18–20 different fabrics are ideal)

#10 crochet thread

Doll sewing needle

CUTTING

Base Fabric

Cut the base square 40˝ × 40˝.

Triangle Points

Cut 4 squares 5˝ × 5˝ for the center layer.

Cut 6 squares 5˝ × 5˝ for the second layer.

Cut 8 squares 5˝ × 5˝ for the third layer.

Cut 2–10 additional squares 5˝ × 5˝ per layer for each subsequent layer.

Binding Fabric

Cut 5 strips 3¼˝ × width of fabric.

Construction

1. Following the Basic Technique instructions (page 81), create a 40˝ × 40˝ pinecone block. *Note: The quilt will be heavy by the time you reach the edges.*

2. Stitch together the 5 binding strips and cut 4 strips 3¼˝ × 43˝. Bind each edge following the Binding instructions (page 84).

3. Your Pinecone baby quilt is complete.

Rather than displaying in a crib, consider using a smaller version of this quilt to show off a vase of flowers.

Pretty Pinecone Corsage

FINISHED CORSAGE: 3½″

Don't limit your projects to home decor—wear your fabulous folk art pieces to add a little wow to your outfit. These corsages are great starter projects because they are fast to finish, and they also make great gifts!

MATERIALS

Yardages are based on fabric 40″ wide.

Base fabric: 1 square 5″ × 5″ fabric of your choice

Backing: 1 square 5″ × 5″

Binding: 1 square 16″ × 16″

Triangle points: ⅓ yard assorted fabric scraps

Cotton thread

Hand sewing needle

Sew-on pin back

CUTTING

Base Fabric

Cut the base square 5″ × 5″.

Backing Fabric

Cut the backing square 5″ × 5″.

Triangle Points

Cut 60–80 squares 2″ × 2″.

Binding Fabric

Cut the 16″ × 16″ square in half along the diagonal. From one of the halves, subcut a bias strip 17″ × 2½″.

Construction

1. Following the Basic Technique instructions (page 81), use the 2″ × 2″ squares to create a pinecone block using the 5″ base fabric. When your pinecone reaches the edges of the base fabric, stop. You do not need to finish the corners for this project.

2. Trim the piece in a circular pattern, making sure not to clip any of the stitches holding down your triangles.

3. Cut the backing fabric in a circle to place over the stitches on the base fabric. Baste in place around the edges.

4. Bind using the Binding instructions (page 84), except stitch the bias strips around the circle with a ½″ seam allowance. Tuck under the raw edges at the end.

5. Use a needle and thread to stitch on the sew-in pin back.

6. Your corsage is now ready to wear.

Striking Pinecone Hoop Wall Art

FINISHED SIZE: 18˝ diameter

Give a folk finish to your folk art by framing this wall hanging in an quilting hoop for display. If you are even more intrepid, use a larger base cloth and whip up a table cover to add flair to any room.

MATERIALS

Yardages are based on fabric 40″ wide.

Base fabric: ⅝ yard lightweight cotton or muslin

Triangle points: 2–3 yards assorted prints and solids

#10 crochet thread

Doll needle

18″ quilting hoop

Optional: ¾ yard coordinating fabric for binding

CUTTING

Base Fabric

Cut the base square 22″ × 22″ (the size of the hoop plus 4″).

Triangle Points

Cut 4 squares 4″ × 4″ for the center layer.

Cut 6 squares 4″ × 4″ for the second layer.

Cut 8 squares 4″ × 4″ for the third layer.

Cut 2–10 additional squares 4″ × 4″ per layer for each subsequent layer.

Optional Binding

Cut 1 square 22″ × 22″. Cut the square in half diagonally and subcut 3¼″ bias strips to make 71″ of bias binding.

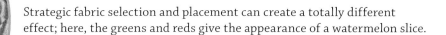

Strategic fabric selection and placement can create a totally different effect; here, the greens and reds give the appearance of a watermelon slice.

Construction

1. Following the Basic Technique instructions (page 81), prepare the base fabric.

2. Place the quilting hoop on the base fabric with the safety pin at the center of the hoop. Lightly trace the inside of the hoop onto the base fabric.

3. Continue following the Basic Technique instructions (page 81) and create a pinecone piece. Stop when your triangles reach the line you drew in Step 2.

4. Test the placement of the quilt in the hoop and ensure the piece will fit. Sometimes, you may need to add another layer so the base fabric does not show.

5. Add the second ring of the hoop over the quilt and tighten the screw. If necessary, use a needle and thread to secure the base fabric corners and excess fabric to the back of the piece.

6. The piece is now ready for hanging.

ROUND PINECONE
TABLE COVER VARIATION

If you prefer not to hang your piece on a wall, you can create a striking centerpiece or table cover. Simply trim the excess base fabric and add the binding strips. Stitch the binding strips together to make 1 long strip. Follow the Binding instructions (page 84), except stitch the bias strip around the circle. Tuck under the raw edges at the end.

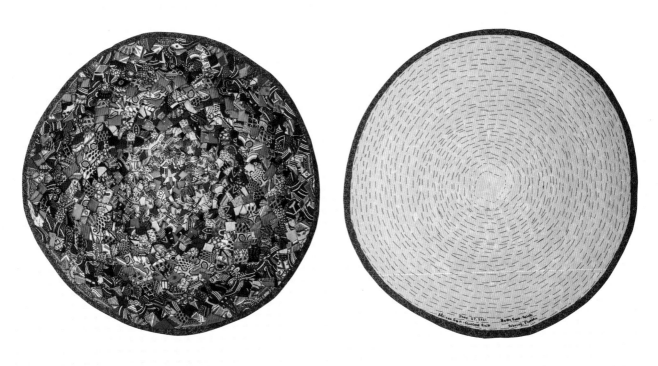

Gee's Bend–Inspired Patchwork Pine Burr Quilt

FINISHED BLOCK: 18″ × 18″ • FINISHED QUILT: 55″ × 55″

My trip to Gee's Bend and the quilts of Lucy Mingo inspired me to
try my hand at a Pine Burr quilt. The nine Pine Burr inset circles use
smaller 4″ × 4″ squares of fabric for the triangles for a more delicate look
without the painstaking effort of using Lucy's even tinier triangles.

MATERIALS

Yardages are based on fabric 40˝ wide.

Base fabric: 1 yard lightweight cotton or muslin

Block fabric: 2¾ yards coordinating prints (optional: 36 precut squares 10˝ × 10˝)

Triangle points: 11–13 yards assorted prints and solids

Backing: 3½ yards

Binding: ¾ yards

Batting: 63˝ × 63˝

#10 crochet thread

Doll needle

Sewing thread

Hand sewing needle

18˝ quilting hoop (optional)

CUTTING

Base Fabric

Cut 9 pieces of lightweight cotton or muslin 10˝ × 10˝ for the pinecone bases.

Block Fabrics

Cut 36 pieces 10˝ × 10˝
(if not using precut squares).

Triangle Points

Cut 4 squares 4˝ × 4˝ for the center layer.

Cut 6 squares 4˝ × 4˝ for the second layer.

Cut 8 squares 4˝ × 4˝ for the third layer.

Cut 2–10 additional squares 4˝ × 4˝ per layer for each subsequent layer.

Binding Fabric

Cut 7 strips 3¼˝ × width of fabric..

Construction

Create the Pine Burr Circles

1. Following the Basic Technique instructions (page 81), prepare the base fabrics. With the safety pins in the center, mark an 8˝ circle on each base fabric piece.

2. Continue following the Basic Technique instructions (page 81) to create 9 pinecone pieces 8˝ × 8˝. There is no need to continue to the edges of the base fabrics, and you do not need to finish the corners. Do not trim.

Create the Blocks

1. Using a ½″ seam allowance, stitch 4 block squares together with sewing thread and a hand sewing needle to create a larger square.

2. Using the template provided, below, mark a 6″ circle in the center of each large block.

3. Cut the center circle out of the block.

4. Clip the edges of the inside of the circle, making sure not to clip more than a scant ½″. Turn the edges under and press down.

5. Place the pine burr circles inside the open circles of your blocks from the bottom and pin them in place. Hand sew the circles into your blocks using regular sewing thread and a running stitch. Remove the pins.

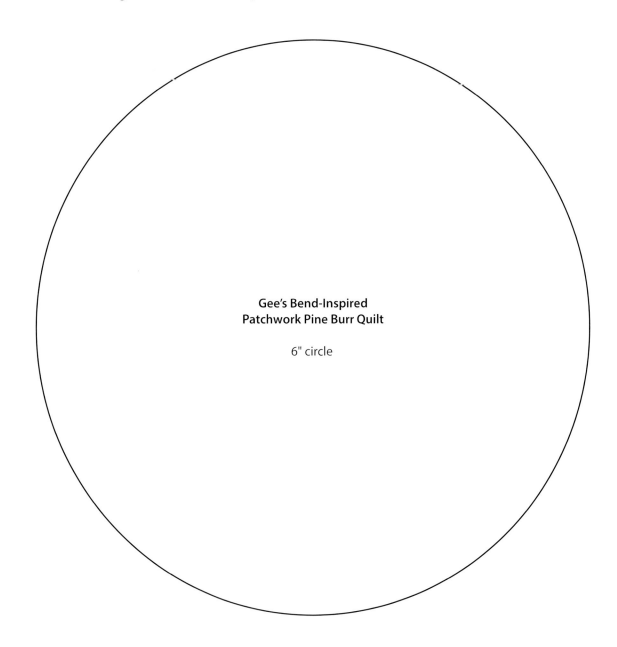

**Gee's Bend-Inspired
Patchwork Pine Burr Quilt**

6" circle

Create the Quilt

1. Using a ½″ seam allowance, sew all the squares together with sewing thread and a hand sewing needle. Your quilt top is now finished.

2. Create a quilt sandwich by layering the backing fabric (face down), the quilt batting, and the quilt top (face up). Smooth out to remove any wrinkles. Pin in place.

3. Using crochet thread and a doll needle, quilt around the pine burr circle 3–4 times to secure the quilt layers together and add a decorative touch to the quilt front. If desired, use a quilting hoop for this step.

4. Repeat for the remaining pine burr circles.

Finish the Quilt

1. Square up the quilt top and trim any excess fabric or batting from the edges.

2. Stitch the 7 binding strips together and subcut into 4 strips 3¼″ × 58″.

3. Follow the steps in the Binding instructions (page 84).

4. Your quilt is complete.

Further Reading

Books

Alma Thomas by Ian Berry and Lauren Haynes (Prestel, 2016)

Always There: The African-American Presence in American Quilts by Cuesta Benberry (University of Pennsylvania Press, 1991)

Black Art Ancestral Legacy: The African Impulse in African-American Art by Alvia J. Wardlaw (Dallas Museum of Art, 1990)

Flash of the Spirit: African and Afro-American Art and Philosophy by Robert Farris Thompson (Vintage, 1984)

Florida Quilts by Charlotte Allen Williams (University Press of Florida, 1992)

The Freedom Quilting Bee: Folk Art and the Civil Rights Movement in Alabama by Nancy Callahan (Fire Ant Books, 2005)

"Introduction: The Quilts of Gee's Bend" by Alvia Wardlaw, in *The Quilts of Gee's Bend* (Tinwood Books, 2002)

The Lumbee by Adolph L. Dial (Chelsea House Publishing, 1993)

A Piece of My Soul: Quilts by Black Arkansans by Cuesta Benberry (University of Arkansas Press, 2000)

Southern Quilts: Celebrating Traditions, History, and Designs by Mary W. Kerr (Schiffer, 2018)

Whizz Bang: Adventures with Folded Fabric Quilts by Racheldaisy (Quiltmania, 2019)

Other Resources

"History and Culture," The Lumbee Tribe (lumbeetribe.com/history-and-culture)

"Material Truths: The Quilts of Gee's Bend at the Whitney Museum of Art, An Exhibition Review" by Michael J. Prokopow (Winterthur Portfolio, Volume 38, Number 1, Spring 2003)

The Museum of the Southeast American Indian (uncp.edu/resources/museum-southeast-american-indian)

"The Quilts of Gee's Bend: A Slideshow" by Rebecca Gross (National Endowment for the Arts, 2015, arts.gov/stories/blog/2015/quilts-gees-bend-slideshow)

Souls Grown Deep (soulsgrowndeep.org)

About the Author

Betty Ford-Smith was born in New Rochelle, New York. She was raised and schooled in Mount Vernon and New Rochelle, New York. Betty is a graduate of the Ophelia DeVore School of Charm and Modeling, New Rochelle Academy, Bennett College in Millbrook, New York, Bard College, State University of New York in New Paltz, and the University of South Carolina. She has lived and worked in New York; St. Thomas, U.S. Virgin Islands; South Carolina; and Florida. She was a teacher and school administrator for 38 years. She loves antiques and has a large collection of African-American Art, African Art, Haitian Art, dolls, and quilts. Her husband, Butler H. Smith Jr., has been very helpful and supportive with all her endeavors.

Betty continues to share the tradition by traveling to teach the Pinecone technique and exhibiting her quilts.

Pinecone Quilts is Betty Ford-Smith's first book.

Visit Betty online and follow on social media!
Website: pineconequilts.com

Photo by Karla Respress